Walking with God
and Other Cycle A Sermons for Proper 23 through Thanksgiving

Based on the First Readings of the Revised Common Lectionary

Argile Smith

CSS Publishing Co., Inc.
Lima, Ohio

WALKING WITH GOD

FIRST EDITION
Copyright © 2011
by CSS Publishing Co., Inc.

Library of Congress Cataloging-in-Publication Data
Smith, Argile Asa, 1955-
    Walking with God : and other Cycle A sermons for Proper 23 through Thanksgiving ; based on the first readings of the Revised common lectionary / Argile Smith. -- 1st ed.
        p. com.
    ISBN 0-7880-2630-5 (alk. paper)
    1. Pentecost--Sermons. 2. Thanksgiving--Sermons. 3. Church year sermons. 4. Common lectionary (1992) I. Title.

BV61.S65 2010
252'.64--dc22   2010040630

ISBN-13: 978-0-7880-2630-0
ISBN-10: 0-7880-2630-5   PRINTED IN USA

*Dedicated to
my lovely and loving congregation
First Baptist Church
Biloxi, Mississippi*

Table of Contents

Proper 23   7
Pentecost 21
Ordinary Time 28
When God Tests Us
Exodus 32:1-14

Proper 24   15
Pentecost 22
Ordinary Time 29
On Speaking Terms
Exodus 33:12-23

Proper 25   23
Pentecost 23
Ordinary Time 30
Going Home
Deuteronomy 34:1-12

Proper 26   31
Pentecost 24
Ordinary Time 31
Who's the Real Leader?
Joshua 3:7-17

Reformation Day   39
When God Does Something New
Jeremiah 31:31-34

All Saints   47
The Lamb
Revelation 7:9-17

Proper 27   **55**
Pentecost 25
Ordinary Time 32
Choosing
Joshua 24:1-3a, 14-25

Proper 28   **63**
Pentecost 26
Ordinary Time 33
Powerless People
Judges 4:1-7

Christ the King   **71**
Proper 29
God Cares
Ezekiel 34:11-16, 20-24

Thanksgiving Day   **79**
Thanksgivings to Remember
Deuteronomy 8:7-18

Proper 23
Pentecost 21
Ordinary Time 28
Exodus 32:1-14

When God Tests Us

When we get nervous about the unknown, we can make mountains out of mole hills. But we aren't by ourselves. Loads of people down through history have made the same mistake.

Take the Israelites, for example. God had delivered them from Egyptian bondage through a series of mystifying miracles at the hand of Moses. Then Moses led them on a three-month journey to Mount Sinai. There God called Moses to the top of the mountain for a meeting with him. Soon Moses came down from the mountain with the Ten Commandments. In due time, God called Moses back to the mountain, and there he remained for forty days and nights (Exodus 24:18).

Moses had become the central figure of stability for the Israelites. After all, he had been the leader of God's people even before they were set free from Egyptian bondage. They had grown to lean heavily on him. His presence among them became absolutely essential. As long as he was nearby, they felt safe. If they couldn't see him, especially for a long period of time, they apparently began to get nervous. That's when they started to jump to conclusions. A mountain soon formed from a mole hill.

According to Exodus, Moses left the people to go up the mountain for an extended meeting with God. He didn't come down from the mountain soon enough; so they started to wonder if he would return at all. They could see the fire on the mountain where he was meeting with God, but they couldn't see him. In fact, they hadn't seen him for several days. Jittery, they began to think that he wouldn't ever return to them. They may have convinced themselves that the fire had consumed him, leaving them all alone.

Like all of us, the Israelites craved a relationship with God. They showed their eagerness to devote themselves to God by signing on immediately to worship Him alone and to live according to his ways (Exodus 24:3). Once Moses presented the Ten Commandments to them, they immediately agreed to live by them. They seemed to be enthusiastic about following the one true God, their deliverer. Just as quickly, they appeared to be eager to ditch God once his messenger disappeared without a trace and to replace him with another deity.

And like all of us, the Israelites confused silence with absence. They hadn't heard from God or Moses, his messenger, in a while. Consequently, they figured that God must have left the mountain and Moses must have died there, leaving his people waiting anxiously in the middle of an unforgiving desert. In their anxiety, they wondered who would take them on from there.

How do you react when God seems to give you the silent treatment? Do you assume that he's absent? If so, what do you do about it?

Poor Aaron didn't help the tense situation very much, even though he tried. He gave his best effort to keeping the people focused on their commitment to God, but to no avail. Aaron had been with Moses from the start, and he himself had witnessed in Egypt and Sinai, and every place in between, the miracle-working power and the all-sufficient presence of God. He seemed to know that the silence on the mountain didn't mean God had made an exit. Apparently he couldn't convey that confidence to the people who had already jumped to the conclusion that Moses would never return to them.

At the same time, however, he knew the people whom God had delivered from Egypt. They had been raised in slavery. They had lost a part of themselves somewhere in the brutal treatment they had received at the hands of their oppressors. The Egyptians had conditioned them to be afraid. You could imagine that faith wouldn't come easily to them. Aaron knew that something had to be done to assuage their fear. If he didn't try something, they would jump ship on him just as quickly as they bailed out on the God who used him and Moses to get them this far on their journey to the promised land.

They wanted Aaron to help them get on with their lives so they could move forward from there. Taking that step meant crafting a deity that would give them a measure of comfort. They had grown accustomed to the Egyptian idols that they could see and touch. Aaron told them the cost for that kind of god would be high, but they didn't mind paying it. Desperate, they displayed nothing less than blind allegiance to the hope that Aaron could craft a god for them to worship. They ripped the gold jewelry from their bodies and their clothing so Aaron could boil it down into a deity. They decided that their healthy appetite for a relationship with God could be satisfied with the junk food of an idol. What they didn't know was that their devotion to their new deity would turn out to be the source of unimaginable pain for them.

So Aaron crafted a god for them, and they fell in love with it immediately. It probably looked like something they could relate to from their days in Egypt. The golden calf that Aaron crafted from their jewelry brought back memories of home, even if home had bad memories. It made them feel as if they had something worthwhile to which they could devote themselves. Gazing upon it, they didn't feel so alone in the desert.

When Aaron saw that the people had glued themselves to the idol he constructed, he tried to direct their attention back to the living God who Moses was talking with upon the mountain. When he finished the golden calf, he built an altar for it, and he proclaimed the next day as a festival. But he decreed that the festival would be in honor to the living Lord (v. 5). Perhaps he thought that a festival to the living God would lure the people back to him, even though he would have to share the billing with the idol they really wanted to worship.

What Aaron tried to do has been given a name. Scholars call it syncretism. It's the effort made to blend different perspectives so everyone can work together to accomplish a common goal. Some theorists like to refer to it as fusion. It's like melting the wax on two candles, pouring the liquid into one mold that shapes it into something else. It's like taking various bits of gold jewelry, melting them, pouring the liquid gold into a new mold and letting it harden into a new form that everyone can appreciate. It's like taking a relationship with God and melting it with devotion to a cold, dead deity to form something that would be appealing to everyone.

For Aaron, the effort at syncretism didn't work. It rarely does for anyone else either. Jesus told us as much when he warned us not to put new wine into old wineskins. The new wine of a living relationship with Christ can't ever be contained in the old wineskin of dead religion for very long.

We tend to look at the Israelites in this episode of their journey with at least a hint of disgust. Such a perspective on their huge blunder would be easy to develop. We say they should have known better, and Aaron should have known better. Before we cast judgment on what he and the others did on that sad day, we do well to see that what happened to them can happen to God's people at any time in history.

Even now we may find ourselves so eager to see God at work that we take matters usually left to him into our own hands. Or, like Aaron, we try to harmonize the life we have with the Lord with the ways of a culture that eventually has us wandering farther and farther away from him.

That's what happened to the Israelites. They wandered far away from God. From the way they behaved, you wondered if they would ever return to him. Instead of worshiping the true and living God, they turned their attention to praying at the altar of the deity they had made for themselves. Strangely enough, their devotion to their idol led them down the path of self-indulgence after they affirmed that they would take the high road of walking with God in obedience and love.

Was the Lord surprised by what they had done? Not one bit. Disappointed? Yes, but not surprised. It's as if he left them alone so who they really were would rise to the surface. In the silence that accompanied Moses' departure to the mountaintop, his people got a chance to take the high road of commitment to him when he didn't seem to be around every day to remind them that he was watching them. You may even say that he set up the crisis to see how they would react. He wasn't surprised with their reaction to his silence. They took it to mean that he was absent and decided to take matters into their own hands.

It wasn't the first time God's people reacted that way, and it wouldn't be the last. Even today we find ourselves reacting like God's people then. If he doesn't show up every once in a while and remind us constantly of his presence among us, we get the impression that we can go our own way and that no one will care or even notice.

God's silence tests our mettle. When he doesn't seem to be giving attention to us, it presents for us a crisis, a crisis of faith. Will we move forward and trust him? Or will we decide that we would do just as well to take action on our own behalf?

Meanwhile, up on the mountain, God tested Moses too. He didn't test Moses like a research specialist would test a laboratory mouse in order to prove a scientific theory. No. God tested Moses like a dad tested his daughter by giving her the keys to his car. All finished with the driver's education classes and having passed the driver's test, she had a brand new license that was burning a hole in her purse. She was itching to get out on the open road by herself, so her dad let her take his car for a spin around the neighborhood. Before he put the keys in her hands, he said, "Sweetheart, don't go over the speed limit."

"I won't," she said with her eyes glued to the keys in his hand.

"And don't let anyone ride in the car with you."

"All right, Dad."

"And be back home in one hour."

"I will." Then she grabbed the keys from him, kissed him on his cheek, and out the door she went with the parting words, "I love you, dad!" resonating through the house as she made her way through the front door.

Her dad tested her that day. After he provided the necessary training and gave her sufficient instruction, he let her go on her own to see how she would react. He didn't test her because he wanted to conduct research on teenagers behind the wheel. He tested her because he loved her and wanted her to enjoy the liberty that driving would give her and to take seriously the responsibility associated with the freedom he had given her. Because he had reared her, he knew how she would handle the test he had placed before her. But nothing made his heart swell with pride like the front door swinging open 45 minutes later and his daughter bounding into the house, hugging him again, and thanking him for letting her drive his car. Her trip through the neighborhood had gone extremely well she said with a smile on her face. Her dad smiled, too, because she had passed the test.

God gave Moses the keys to the Israelite nation and said, "It's yours to drive. Ditch it if you want. Trade it in if you want. Let me know what you decide." All the while God knew how Moses would react, so he wasn't surprised when Moses pleaded with him to give the people he had delivered from bondage another chance. Neither was he surprised when Moses said that saving them would speak well of him in the land. And after all, his reputation among his people mattered more than anything else. God must have smiled when Moses passed the critical test of leadership. He loved God's people just as God himself loved them. Like his Lord, he didn't want to give up on them. Too much was at stake.

You may be thinking that God testing Moses was cruel. You may insist that he could find a better way to guide his people along toward the promised land. Or you may be taking the whole testing issue one step farther by insisting that you shouldn't be tested. The notion of God testing you insults you; your intelligence, your devotion, and your sincerity.

Tests aren't meant to be mean-spirited attempts to make our lives miserable. Tests are necessary. Without tests, how would we know that we have made progress? Suppose we decided that tests shouldn't be given to students. How would we know if third-graders have made progress with their math skills? How would we be able to evaluate the extent to which a high-school senior could read or write well enough to function productively in society? How would a soldier in boot camp know if he or she has mastered the skills necessary to move forward in the field of battle? In Christian living, how will we know that we have matured enough to take on the challenges that await us as we make our own journey to the promised land of a deep and abiding relationship with the Lord?

And what about our obligation to other believers? My journey with Christ isn't just about me, and your journey with him isn't just about you. It's about them too. It's about the others who join us, who don't know the way as well as we. It's about leading them to stay strong in the days when God is silent. It's about holding on to the promise that just because he's silent, we can't conclude that he's absent. It's about helping them to see that they're asking for trouble when they think about bailing out on God in favor of another way that seems to make sense at the moment.

So welcome the tests that God brings our way. He's not trying to hurt us. He's trying to help us so we will be fit for the journey called living. Through Jesus Christ, we have been given eternal life. When God tests us along the way, it's to help us stay on track so we can experience his fulfillment in our relationship with him. Amen.

Proper 24
Pentecost 22
Ordinary Time 29
Exodus 33:12-23

On Speaking Terms

Do you ever have moments in your life when you feel that God must have decided somehow not to be on speaking terms with you anymore? Maybe you haven't seen him answer your prayers for some time, or perhaps you haven't sensed his presence in your life for a while. For some reason, you have been led to wonder if he's giving you a cold shoulder. You begin to think that he has stopped talking with you altogether.

If you can say that such a thought has crossed your mind, then you can probably identify with the dilemma faced by God's people in the story recorded in Exodus 33. They had to contend with God's silent treatment when he stopped talking with them. After what they had done, we really can't blame God for distancing himself from them. They had insulted him and the covenant he had made with them by wasting no time before they gave themselves to worshiping a golden calf at the foot of Mount Sinai. Moses had gone up the mountain to meet with God about the Ten Commandments, and his people waited only a little while before they decided that their leader would never return. They took matters into their own hands and crafted a deity that made them feel comfortable in the loneliness of the desert. No wonder God refused to give any assurance that he wouldn't go any farther with them. He said to Moses that he would provide an angel to guide them on the rest of their journey to the promised land, but he could not say that he would go himself (vv. 33:1-3). Indeed, God and his people were no longer on speaking terms.

God's relationship with Moses was completely different. They talked to each other like two old trusted, lifelong friends (v. 11). They seemed to enjoy each others' company, and everyone in the camp knew it. The people knew when Moses would make his way to his conversation with God. They would watch Moses pass on his way to the tent of meeting, and silence filled the camp when he passed. Out of respect for Moses and fear for God, they stood to their feet when he passed their way. They knew better than to show any form of disrespect.

Once inside the tent, Moses and God talked with each other. They may have taken up their conversation from the previous day. Friends glad to see each other, perhaps they visited about nothing special or maybe they took on some fairly prickly issues. And like friends who were close to one another, they probably talked about everything. No topic was off limits between them.

While we lament that sometimes we feel like the children of Israel to whom God has given a cold shoulder, we find comfort in the fact that he would rather talk with us like friends. Jesus said as much when he shared with his disciples that he saw them as his friends and not slaves (John 15:14-15). For us as believers in the twenty-first century, an intimate relationship with him can be the norm and not the exception. When we grow in our walk with Jesus, we can think about our relationship with him in terms of friendship; we can become more confident about talking with him about what really matters to us. To borrow some of Paul's words, we can make our requests known to God (Philippians 4:6). Or like John said, we can have the confidence in knowing that he hears us when we pray (1 John 13-14). We can talk with him about anything and everything.

In his deep and abiding friendship with the Lord, Moses made a serious request. He appealed to the Lord, "Show me your ways" (v. 13). We can understand why Moses would make such a daring request. He wanted to know what God expected of him and the people who had followed him out of Egypt. He seemed to be asking God, "Show me your intentions." If Moses only knew what God had in mind for them and what he wanted them to do, he would lead the people to do it.

Up to that point, Moses didn't know what to do next with God's people. God had told him that he didn't think he would go with them any farther. They had been obstinate. Their stiff necks kept them from bowing their heads and hearts and submitting themselves to God and honoring the covenant they had recently made with him.

That's why Moses appealed to God as a friend. He put all of his chips on the table, so to speak, in his appeal for God. He asked God to show him once and for all what God expected of his people. Doing what God wanted would get them out of the desert and on their way to the land he promised them.

In his appeal, Moses brought up the fact that the Lord favored him, so his request for divine insight had a dependable foundation. It was based on their rock-solid relationship. Furthermore, Moses went on to say, the Israelites under his care still belonged to the Almighty. They needed his guidance or they wouldn't make it to the next rest stop in the desert, much less to the promised land. Slaves in a foreign land for all of their lives, they would have to grow into their status as God's chosen people.

True to his nature, the Lord didn't hold a grudge against Moses or the people. He responded favorably to Moses' request. And he did something else. In a way, he told Moses, "You want me to give you a map, but I would rather give you a guide."

That's something to think about as we take a look at our friendship with God. Like Moses, we would like for God simply to tell us what God expects of us. If we know what

God wants us to do, we will do it if at all possible. We want to please him, but we don't know how if he won't tell us. Telling us what he wants us to do would make following him much simpler. Like Moses, therefore, we would like for God to show us his ways.

Sometimes we react to the lack of clarity regarding God's leadership like Fay responded to the supervisor at her new job. She had been at work for a couple of weeks when her supervisor called her into his office for an evaluation.

"First of all," he said with a grin, "I am glad that you are on the team, so don't forget that fact as I talk with you about a problem that I am having with you."

"What problem?" she asked, completely shocked by his remark.

"You're not following through on my directives," he said.

"What directives? You haven't given me one directive ever since I've been here. Yes, you have given me some suggestions and offered a few possibilities for getting my work done more efficiently, but I haven't heard you give a single directive since the first day I walked in the door."

"Well, then, we have misunderstood each other. For me, a suggestion or an idea is a directive."

"Oh, I didn't know," Fay confessed. "Now that I understand, you can count on me to follow through without fail."

"Good. By the way, I have a suggestion about tomorrow's staff meeting."

Once Fay understood what her supervisor expected of her, she could carry out his directives without any problem. In the same way, we would like for God to tell us in simple, straightforward terms what he wants so we can please him by obeying him.

That's where the map comes into the picture. We would like God to give us a map with the path for our journey that

God wants us to take. A map provides clear, unmistakable information for us to follow to get to the destination he has in mind for us.

When we travel abroad, we would be wise to carry a tourist manual that is complete with all kinds of information about the cities we will visit, including maps. We consult the manual every time we turn the corner in search of tourist sights. The map helps us get where we want to go so we can see what we traveled there to see in the first place.

To be honest, most of us probably prefer a tour guide over a map. Instead of stumbling along trying to read the map and see the sights at the same time, following a tour guide can enable us to enjoy the sightseeing adventure more. We simply follow the guide and hear him or her talk about the significant features of the places we visit. We can rest in the assurance that the guide will take us where we need to go and will keep us from places that would be a waste of our time. Who wouldn't prefer a guide over a map?

When we pray, we tend to ask God for a map because it's easy for us to use it in our effort to please him. But he prefers to give us a guide because it makes the journey more rewarding.

Of course, God is the guide. We can rest assured that he will lead us where we need to go, and he will keep us from places that won't be good for us or guide us through them so we can arrive at our destination safe and sound. God goes with us through life, every step of the way, guiding us along and never leaving us for one minute. Like Moses, we enjoy God's abiding presence because he's our friend. In the presence of the Almighty, our souls find rest. We have no apprehension because God is near.

Moses made a second request of God. He asked the Lord, "Show me your glory!" Again, he made a daring request, but he felt confident in making it because nothing was off-limits between him and his God.

We can appreciate Moses' request. God's glory involves his physical presence. Consequently, seeing his glory means seeing him with our eyes. How many times have you wished that you could actually see Jesus in the same way that his disciples saw him? If you could look on his face, listen to his voice, observe his body language, and touch his hand, everything would be better for you. The questions that have gone unanswered so far could be put to God directly. The needs that you have could be brought to his attention instantly. You could hear for yourself God's answer and watch him actually take care of the need that you brought to him. Probably most important, you could feel God's gentle touch as he placed his loving hand on your shoulder or hugged you in his strong arms. His physical presence with us would make following God easier.

It wouldn't be best for us. Like Moses, we can't see God's face and live. To see God's face means to behold what lies ahead of us. Frankly, if we knew all of what's ahead of us, we would probably die of shock!

No, God doesn't show us where we're going, but he lets us see where he's been. By the same token, he's not always going to let us see what lies ahead, but he'll point out how he walked with us in the past. That's what the Lord seemed to be saying to Moses. He told him, and us by inference, "I won't show you my glory, but I will let you see my goodness."

All of us have seen God's goodness to us in our lives when we look for it. Like he said to Moses, we have seen his integrity at work. His name stands out as wonderful indeed. And we have also seen God's mercy, love, and grace reflected in a number of ways. Of course, the central expression of these great virtues centers in Jesus Christ. God's Son will always demonstrate that he keeps his word and upholds his wonderful name. Likewise, Jesus Christ will forever reflect in a superlative way the Lord's great mercy and grace to us.

Indeed we have seen the most perfect expression of God's goodness in Christ.

Notice something else the Lord did for Moses. It's something that reflected well on his character (vv. 21-23). Remember that Moses wanted to see the Lord's glory. Honoring Moses request would have been a dangerous proposition. However, the Lord really wanted Moses to experience God in an up-close-and-personal kind of way. Such an intimate encounter would benefit Moses for many years to come. For that reason, the Lord encouraged Moses to come a little closer to him. He went on to say to his friend, "Stand here close to me, and I will protect you."

As Moses moved next to the Lord's side, he felt God's hand directing him to a cleft in the rock that served like a cradle. There God placed his friend for his protection. Like a baby tucked safely into a cradle by a caring and loving parent, the Lord placed Moses in the cleft of the rock. Then God's mighty hand covered him. When his glory passed by, no harm would come to Moses.

What's the most striking part of the scene for you? For me, it's when God told Moses, "Come here and stand by me" and then placing him gently in the cleft of the rock and covering him with his hand.

That portion of the scene raises an important question. How often does the Almighty invite us to come close, to make our way to him, to stand by his side so he can watch out for us? When we come close, we find in God's presence that we can trust him. We can trust him to place His mighty, gentle hand over us to hold us close. He calls us to come close so God can protect us in his mighty hand.

The story of Moses, God's friend, encourages us. Through it we get a clear picture of how much God wants us to know him intimately. Granted, he expects us to come to him on his terms, not ours. But his terms always serve us best in the long run. By coming to God and learning to trust him, we come to comprehend how much he wants to guide us, how good he is to us, and how much he wants us to come close to him.

What does this story have to say to us when we feel that God's not on speaking terms with us? It assures us that God doesn't hold grudges and that he's always willing to open his arms wide to us. What's even more beautiful, he's waiting for us to take that important step. In fact, he may have been waiting for some time now, so don't put God off any longer. He wants to hide you in the cleft of the rock and cover you with his hand. Amen.

Going Home

At the end of a long trip, home always looks appealing! Turning the corner and seeing the house you left days or weeks earlier can sometimes provide the best snapshot of the whole trip. The word *home* has a pleasant ring to it, and it's a particularly beautiful word to hear after being away from it for a while.

While such an assertion makes sense after a weeklong vacation at a theme park, it makes even more sense after the long journey called life. For Christians, coming to the end of life's journey doesn't have to prompt a sense of dread and fear. Because of what we know about God's love for us and his gift of eternal life in heaven, the end of our journey here can foster an invigorating awareness that home's just around the corner.

Deuteronomy 34 gives us the moving story of Moses when he went home at the end of his journey. He had finished his life's work. What a life he lived! Neatly divided into three segments, each spanning forty years, Moses' life included growing up in Egyptian royalty, working as a shepherd in the wilderness, and serving as the leader of God's people from slavery to liberty.

The last forty years of his life had been most eventful. From the day his curiosity drew him to a burning bush until the last day alive, he had been on quite a remarkable journey. He heard God call him to a task that he knew he could never complete by himself. God showed him along the way that God could be trusted. He would give Moses what he couldn't give himself to finish the work to which he had been called. Accordingly, Moses got to hear Pharaoh give the order to let God's people go so they could leave Egypt. He got to watch as God's people worshiped him through the first Passover meal in preparation for the journey across the desert to the promised land. He got to see God separate the Red Sea so the people could cross over into safety. On the freedom side of the Red Sea, he had the rare and — many times — painful privilege of beholding God as he worked with his people to grow them into the holy nation God knew they could become. He got to be a part of such a grand transformation project that would forever be heralded as one of God's greatest miracles. By using Moses, God delivered his people from bondage and guided them to the promised land. A remarkable journey for Moses, but now it was coming to an end. Soon he would be going home.

According to the story, God took him to a mountain so he could get a good look at the land he had promised his people generations earlier. You could say that it was a fitting place to end his work. Interestingly enough, his work started on a mountain, so ending it on a mountain seemed to be appropriate. From his perch on the mountain, Moses got to see the land that God would give to his people. First Moses looked north, then west, and finally south in order to take in all of what God planned to give the children of Israel. Moses must have felt a sense of accomplishment as he soaked in what God showed him.

Some people would say that Moses probably felt that God cheated him out of the joy of crossing over with the people into the land. After all, he had poured out his life in leading them across the desert, which turned out to be a forty-year obligation. The best part of the journey involved what happened at the beginning of it. When the people determined that they couldn't take the land early on in the journey, God led them back into the desert to die. Doing so would give the next generation an opportunity to obey him as courageous followers who would be loyal to him. In the meantime, Moses had the heavy responsibility for keeping the nation focused until the next generation would be ready to take the land.

Even though he remained loyal throughout the four decades of his leadership, the Lord disqualified him from going into the land himself. According to Deuteronomy 1:34-39, God decreed that nobody in Moses' generation would enter the promised land because fear of the obstacles to taking it paralyzed them (see Numbers 13-14). In God's decree, he mentioned Moses by name. Like everyone else except Joshua and Caleb, Moses passed on the opportunity to speak up for God and to encourage the people to take a step of faith forward into the promised land. Because his fear paralyzed his tongue, he would have to suffer along with everyone else in his generation.

God's ways defy explanation at times, but so does his goodness. For Moses, not being able to make his home in the land flowing with milk and honey must have certainly disappointed him. He tried to get God to change his mind about his decree, but to no avail. Not only did God turn down his request, but he also told Moses not to bring it up ever again (Deuteronomy 3:23-29). Years later, however, being able to go to the home God prepared for him must have exhilarated him. Across the years, perhaps Moses had a change of heart when he thought about the location of his home.

Helen looked forward to going home. She lived in the house that she and her husband had built in 1964, but the home she had in mind was in heaven with her husband. She and Bobby had been married for 55 years when he passed away suddenly just a year or so earlier. Ever since his death, she talked about the glad day when she would be able to see him again in heaven. When she talked about heaven, she described in rich detail the features of a home that Bobby would appreciate. For that reason, she described lavish scenery with flowers and shrubs in perennial bloom. Bobby loved gardening. So for her, going to heaven meant living in a cottage near a superbly manicured garden full of budding trees and flowering shrubs. That's where she would find Bobby in heaven, and that's where she wanted to go. She could hardly wait to get there.

Ben's mom suffered from a form of dementia that got noticeably worse not long after she celebrated her eightieth birthday. He watched her forget where she had put her glasses, and then in due time she forgot how to use glasses altogether. The pride and joy of her life, her grandchildren and great-grandchildren, somehow faded away in her mind. She couldn't remember their names at first, and over time she didn't know them at all.

She could always remember the home of her childhood. She would often talk about her mom and dad, her brothers and sisters, and the good times they had at home together. Before long, she got concerned about her parents, who had died decades earlier. Ben would catch her gathering up her belongings and heading for the front door. He would ask her where she was going in such a hurry. Every time he asked, she would give the same reply, "I'm going home so I can see Mama and Papa. I need to check on them." She missed her parents, and she longed to see them again. Consequently, nothing would have pleased her more than being able to go home.

For Moses and all of God's people, when we get ready to go home, nothing else really seems to matter. From that perspective, going home doesn't feel like punishment; it's more like a reward.

Something else about God and his relationship with his people comes to light in the story in Deuteronomy 34 that certainly captures our attention. Notice God's remarkable way of taking care of his choice servants. When the time came for Moses to bring his journey to an end, God didn't vanish from the scene. Quite the opposite, God accompanied Moses to the mountain and stayed with him until he took his last breath. Then God buried Moses' body himself somewhere on the mountain.

God's care for Moses on the mountain makes an important statement about him that we don't want to overlook in his relationship with us. The psalmist affirmed that the Lord considers the death of his children to be precious (Psalm 116:15). We wouldn't be surprised to know that God considers our lives to be precious to him. With our lives we serve God, but what value can a dying person have for God? We can no longer serve him, and we can no longer go out and do what he commands. From our perspective, death doesn't have the same value.

The Lord has a different perspective on the death of his children. We matter to God when life surges within us, and he cares about us just as much life leaks out of us. While we live, we enjoy his presence. When we die, we can count on the blessing of his company then as well. He considers us just as precious in dying as he does when living. Whether living or dying, we are precious in God's sight.

Perhaps the care provided by hospice organizations across the country reflects God's attitude about us when we face death. Hospice caregivers work with terminally ill patients and their families as death approaches. Along with providing medical care to the patient as he or she fades away into eternity, they encourage the family members. They teach them how to treat their loved one with care and dignity. They show how death can be understood as something valuable and a person dying as an individual to be honored and not discarded.

As the story in Deuteronomy 34 also shows us, going home involves leaving a legacy. For Moses, the legacy that lived on after him included what people said about him, his death, and his life among them. What they remembered about him spoke volumes about the man he had become in their eyes.

Did Moses set out to leave a legacy of tremendous accomplishment and unflappable trust in God? Probably not. Follow his footsteps in the stories about him in the Bible, and you draw that conclusion that he didn't care that anyone would remember him. He only wanted to served the Lord by accomplishing the task to which he had been assigned.

Like all young pastors, Brian had his heroes. One of them served as the pastor of a church in Brian's hometown. Brian had watched the church grow deep and wide. In other words, the membership increased steadily across the years, and the members grew spiritually so they could carry out some fairly incredible kingdom tasks together.

When Brian heard that his pastor hero had announced his retirement, he asked for an appointment with him. He wanted to spend a little time with the pastor who had mentored him without even knowing it.

Nervous about meeting his bigger-than-life hero, Brian had some questions written on a note pad that he carried with him into the pastor's office. After a few pleasantries, Brian got right to work, asking one question after the next.

He asked one question in particular that triggered an unexpected answer from his mentor pastor. He asked, "What do you want to be remembered for when it's all said and done?"

"I don't want to be remembered for anything."

Shocked by the reply he received, Brian pressed, "Aren't you concerned about your legacy?"

"Absolutely not. I'm just the messenger of the Lord. I don't want to leave a legacy of my own. I only want to please him with my life."

Perhaps that's how Moses might have felt about all the hullabaloo that accompanied his death. The people of Israel who had followed him all of their lives honored him for his investment in them, but he may not have been so impressed with his life. After all, he knew the mistakes he had made, the shortcomings he had to deal with constantly, and the spiritual and organizational frustrations he experienced along the way as he led God's people to the land God had promised them.

The people certainly didn't see his life and his death that way. For an entire month they grieved his loss. As they grieved, they came to the conclusion that God made a sovereign decision to take Moses home. Otherwise he would have still been alive. Although he was 120 years old, they said to each other, he had the vigor and stamina of a much younger man. Apparently God pulled him out of the picture in keeping with what was best for Moses and God's people.

Maybe that's why God wouldn't give anyone a clue as to where he buried Moses. Who knows what they may have done. If they knew where his body was laid to rest, they may have gone to the spot, exhumed the body, and put it in a tomb. Then they would live with the temptation of venerating his body instead of trusting in the Lord as they stepped into their future.

But listen to them as they talked about Moses after he went home. Imagine what they must have said to one another when they brought up the stories about the man who had finished his work so well.

"Do you remember the time Moses got water out the rock? My dad told me the story more than a few times. He said that Moses was so close to God that he was able to do things like God alone could do them."

"I remember well my grandfather telling me about watching Moses part the Red Sea by calling on the name of the Lord. Papa told me more than once that Moses was one of a kind. He always talked about how God kept the waters back while Moses took the people through to safety."

"I was just a kid when I first heard about Moses. My parents had the greatest respect for him. They said that he was one of God's choice servants, and we were lucky to have him as our leader. They never could get over the way Moses seemed to talk with God like friends carry on a conversation with each other. They could never remember a time when Moses didn't change the atmosphere of a room when he entered it."

All of us will go home one day. Through Jesus Christ, we can look forward to it, and we can rest in the assurance of God's presence when our time comes to leave here and go there. After we're gone, the legacy of a life well lived will be passed along when we live in a way that shows our devotion to him. Amen.

Proper 26
Pentecost 24
Ordinary Time 31
Joshua 3:7-17

Who's the Real Leader?

At an office meeting, Ben got the official news that he would become the manager of one of the most influential departments in the company. His colleagues admired him because of his tireless work, and they respected him as a dependable person in whom they could place their trust. They were glad when they found out that he had gotten the promotion. In order to celebrate the news with him, they bought him a gift. Well, it was actually more like a gag-gift, the kind that he would place on his shelf and chuckle over every time he saw it.

They searched far and wide and finally found the perfect gift for Ben. It was a cap that had two bills sewn onto it instead of one. Both bills faced in opposite directions. A curious caption had been printed around the cap. Bill read it out loud when he took the cap out of the gift bag. He read, "I'm the leader; which way did they go?"

Although the cap was meant to be a joke, it expressed the challenge Ben faced in his new role. Now he was a leader, but how would he get people to follow him? How would he prevent them from going in a hundred different directions at once?

That's a question we ask when we talk about leadership. Mountains of material have been written on the subject of leadership, and loads of conferences have been developed to make people into good leaders. In fact, corporations across the country are eager to do whatever's necessary to instill good leadership skills in their most promising employees.

Because leadership has been the focus of corporate attention, some people think that it's not an important issue for them. They don't ever intend to serve like Ben in a role that demands them to know how to lead others.

But in a way, all of us have to develop good leadership skills. For the sake of our families, our marriages, our personal lives, and our futures, we have to take ownership of decisions that will have an influence on the people around us. In our churches, all of us would do well to learn some lessons in leadership as we carry out kingdom tasks together.

In Joshua, we find an excellent model for effective leadership. Reading through the Bible book that bears his name, you can pick up on some of the traits that made him a good leader. Joshua faced a number of challenges as a young leader who walked in the shadow of Moses. The way Joshua faced them made him an excellent example for leadership.

Joshua's leadership example shows us the value of trusting God with the future. Throughout the story about Israel occupying the promised land, the Lord assured Joshua of God's presence. The young leader certainly needed God's assurance. After all, he walked in the shadow of Moses, whom everyone in Israel had followed all of their lives. Stepping into his leadership role would make any person's knees buckle.

In response to the Lord's assurance, Joshua consistently demonstrated his faithful devotion to God. At the beginning of Joshua's story, for instance, the Lord assured him that he would be successful as he led Israel into Canaan. Joshua showed that he took the Lord's assurance to heart. He immediately carried out the commands that the Lord had given to him. When he followed the Lord's instruction without fail, he would be successful.

Joshua's devotion to the Lord never faded across the years. An example of his lifelong commitment to the Lord involved something that happened near the end of his life.

Having led the people of Israel to occupy the land the Lord had promised them, Joshua finished up his work as their leader. That's when he called them together for one last meeting. He gathered them so he could drive home an important challenge. He wanted to persuade them to remain faithful to the Lord as they settled into their new environment. Then he declared with unswerving personal loyalty to God by declaring that he would lead his family to serve the Lord exclusively. Again, his devotion to the Lord prompted him to lead the people of Israel to consider the example he had set for them in following God.

Joshua's leadership example also demonstrates the necessity of a distinct sense of direction. His commitment to the Lord and God's people served as the source of his crystal-clear sense of direction. The vision of the people of Israel taking the land God had promised them influenced Joshua as he made decisions and directed actions of the people of Israel each step of the way. He believed that God had directed his people to the promised land and had called him to lead them to occupy it. Of course, the clarity of his direction came from God. Such a distinct vision helped Joshua to look into the future to see with confidence what he would lead God's people to accomplish as they worked together.

One important fact should be kept in mind. The Lord didn't give the vision exclusively to Joshua. He also placed God's dream in the minds and hearts of the people of Israel too. Consequently, Joshua didn't have to impose his vision on the resistant people and force them to make it a reality. Quite the contrary, the leader and the followers shared the same vision and worked together to realize it. Joshua led them to live out the vision of taking the promised land that God had given to all of them.

Perhaps Joshua learned the value of a clear sense of direction long before he served as the leader of God's people. Before he led Israel himself, he followed Moses, who had guided the nation to the threshold of the promised land. In the role of a follower, Joshua got to see the benefit of working with a leader who had a clear sense of direction. He probably had come to appreciate the fact that people would follow a leader who demonstrated a sense of certainty about the direction to be taken.

Because Joshua and the people of Israel shared the same vision about their future, they also shared the work necessary to make it a reality. As Israel's leader, Joshua didn't do all the work while everyone else looked on from the sidelines. Instead, he led them to work together. As he led, the people followed, and all of them went in the same direction, sharing the joys and sorrows of moving forward to take the land.

Joshua's leadership example validates the importance of being the kind of person worthy of respect. According to Joshua 4:14, the Lord prompted the people of Israel to see Joshua in the same way they had seen Moses. As a result, they began to see Joshua as a leader to be respected. Of course, respecting Joshua came easily to them after they saw God endorsing his leadership with a miracle. As Joshua led the people to cross the Jordan River, the Lord parted the water so everyone could walk on dry land to the other side (vv. 14-17). By faith, Joshua followed God's instruction by leading the people in the direction that God wanted them all to go. In response, God provided the miracle that showed the connection between Joshua's leadership and God's power. Crossing the river with God's endorsement in the form of a miracle encouraged the people to place their trust in Joshua and follow him wherever he led them in the future.

The respect of the people of Israel for Joshua undoubtedly grew across the years as they observed how much he cared about them. Consistently, he led them in ways that validated his abiding concern for them and what was in their best interest. In everything he led them to do, he never indicated even the slightest interest in getting something for himself at the expense of the people who followed him. Instead, he guided his people with a view toward what would be best for them. By putting what would be best for the people of Israel ahead of what may have been best for him personally, he gained credibility and trust. For the people of Israel, Joshua lived in a way that made them respect him as an authentic servant leader who honestly cared for them.

Joshua's leadership example reminds us of the absolute necessity of courage. Leading such a gigantic crowd of people to accomplish the monumental goal of occupying the promised land required Joshua to take a number of huge risks. In order to address the risks, instead of running from them, Joshua had to exercise tremendous courage. Take as an example the courageous directive that he gave to the people of Israel about Jericho. His method for taking the city involved marching, shouting, and blowing trumpets instead of storming the gates and invading it with drawn swords and spears. A strange strategy, it could have demoralized the people of Israel if it didn't work. But Joshua's method for taking the city had come from the Lord (Joshua 5:1-5). For that reason, he courageously instructed the people of Israel on the details related to God's way of capturing Jericho. And it worked, just like God said.

Joshua's courage also became evident when he had to address a serious internal crisis. The victory in Jericho didn't guarantee the people of Israel the same outcome at Ai. In fact, they suffered a miserable defeat there because someone in the camp had violated God's mandate regarding the treasures found in Jericho (Joshua 6:18). Brokenhearted over the defeat, Joshua heard from the Lord about what to do in order to resolve the crisis. He told Joshua that the individual who had violated God's mandate needed to be confronted. Confrontation would not be easy, but it would be necessary. Courageously, Joshua took immediate action. He led his people to discover the person who had violated

God's mandate and mete out punishment for the crime that had taken such a serious toll on the people of Israel.

Joshua could have chosen not to act with courage in the crisis. He could have overlooked the crime committed and attempted to inspire the people to try one more time to take the city. By acting courageously, however, he addressed the crisis and helped the people to regain their momentum so they could conquer Ai on God's terms.

Observing the character traits of a good leader like Joshua begs some gnawing questions. Who's the real leader in Joshua's story? Could Joshua himself take credit for leading God's people to victory as they occupied the land? In order to answer these kinds of questions, consider Joshua 3:7-17. Therein we gain some insight into how great leaders are really made and who should get the credit for making them. Moreover, we come to understand where to turn when we find ourselves in need of leadership skills that will enable us to be effective as we serve the Lord.

We have already seen the value of courage in a leader. The story in Joshua 3 shows us how God encourages us to take on the obstacles and turn them into challenges. Joshua faced a huge obstacle to leading the people to the land God promised his people. The swollen Jordan River appeared to be impossible to cross. Instead of being afraid of the obstacle, however, Joshua registered extreme courage as he faced it. His trust in the Lord had helped him to muster the courage necessary to do something everyone considered impossible.

God musters courage in his people to take on tough tasks. By affirming that God makes us courageous, we can't imply that he prompts us to be foolhardy. We know the difference between being courageous and being nutty. Being courageous means seeing what needs to be done — obstacles and all — and doing it. That's the essence of courageous leadership, and God's responsible for making his people into courageous leaders.

We have also seen in the story of Joshua that a leader needs to earn the respect of the people who follow him or her. According to the passage, God knew it too, and God determined that he would make Joshua into the kind of leader God's people would be able to respect. Although they affirmed Joshua to occupy the position of leadership left vacant by Moses, they had still had not embraced him as God's chosen leader for the next generation of Israel. That kind of respect would come only when they saw God work through him. For that reason, the Lord took them to the Jordan River where they could participate in a miracle that would reflect well on Joshua as their leader.

Imagine how tension must have filled the air as the people heard Joshua instruct them to cross the Jordan River. They could see for themselves that the river had overflowed. Getting across it would take nothing less than a miracle from God. When the priests stepped into the water, the miracle unfolded before their eyes. The water separated like the Red Sea had parted for their parents and grandparents. Now they could see for themselves that God was going into the promised land with them and Joshua could be trusted to lead the way.

By shaping Joshua into an effective leader and by guiding Israel to respect his leadership, the Lord showed that he could be counted on to be faithful to his people. They needed leadership, and God provided a leader.

Nothing has changed about God since those days. Read the scriptures and you will agree that God made leaders out of an assortment of people. Look into the history of the church and you will observe loads of different individuals through whom God worked to lead his people to accomplish kingdom tasks. Even today, he's shaping people to become leaders. As we worship the God who enabled Joshua to lead Israel across the Jordan River, we can place our trust in him to develop leaders for his church. Perhaps he's working on you at this very moment. You may be insisting that you're not leadership material, but he's not budging. God is relentless in his determination to grow you into an effective leader for his glory.

Take seriously what God's doing in your life. Consider the fact that he's working on you so you can be a leader in your home, in your church, and in your relationships with others at work. The time has come for followers to become leaders. Let God take control of your life so he can nurture in you the qualities that will make you into a present-day Joshua. Amen.

When God
Does Something New

After a prolonged spate of bad news about the national and global economic situation, we welcome good news about the economy, even if it's only a little bit of good news. Likewise, after a long illness, we enjoy hearing our physician tell us that things are going to look up for us soon. And who wouldn't be glad to hear about their child or grandchild striking a winning rhythm at work after an extended season of losses characterized by his or her performance?

Jeremiah welcomed the good news about God's plan for his people. A prophet who grieved for Israel for four decades, Jeremiah had been unsuccessful in his attempt to persuade the leaders to return to the Lord. For his work at preaching faithfully and hopefully about the need for spiritual renewal, he received little more than rejection, humiliation, and persecution. To add insult to injury, he had the unenviable privilege of watching the people suffer the consequences because they didn't heed his warning about God's judgment if they didn't repent. As they marched to captivity in a foreign land, he lamented the fate they had inflicted upon themselves.

So when God told him about a new day and a new covenant with his people coming sometime in the future, Jeremiah's heart must have done backflips! Because of God's promise to do something new among his people, Jeremiah could rest in unabated assurance. Somehow God would restore the broken relationship with his people

Today we call attention to God's new work among his people. In this worship experience, we need to talk about how we have seen God do something new among us for his glory. Of course, the backdrop for our time together is a time in history when God did something new in the life of his people, an episode that we have come to call the Protestant Reformation.

Because of what we have encountered in the New Testament, we affirm that God's new day centered in Jesus Christ, his Son. We rejoice every time we read about John the Baptist's introduction of Jesus as the Lamb of God who takes away the sins of the world. We agree with the individuals who listened to Jesus and remarked that he spoke with authority. Like the folks then, we listen to the words of Jesus and confirm that he speaks out of a firsthand relationship with the Father. He assured us that we could have that kind of relationship with God ourselves through him.

So it has been for us who have given ourselves to Jesus Christ. We rest in the confidence that Christ's death made it possible for us to experience life as God intended from the beginning. His resurrection declares for us that we don't need to be afraid of death. He overcame it, and so will we. Our faith in Christ gives us peace about the future. Eternity with him is our inheritance. We are blessed indeed because God kept his promise of doing something new with his people.

Jeremiah reminds us of the place in which God would do something new. In Jeremiah 31:33, he identified it as the heart. Of course, mentioning the heart in those days meant talking about the center of a person's being, the core of his or her life, the wellspring of life itself. Down in the core of a person's life, God intended to do something new. He intended to plant his law there. Instead of writing it on stone, like he did on Mount Sinai, he would script it in the hearts of the people who followed him. There it would have a definite effect. It would be the beginning of something new.

Has God shown how he can do something new among his people by working their hearts? Absolutely! He has demonstrated the way he can transform a person from inside out. One changed person affects another person until an entire city or country is affected by what God's doing in their hearts.

In the January 12, 2008, issue of *The New York Times*, an article was published about the retirement of a minister. What's interesting about the article was that the minister was the pastor of St. Nicholas Church in Leipzig, Germany. The story in the article recounted something that had happened at the church and in the city on October 9, 1989. What happened then and there reflects well on how God can do something new in the hearts of his people.

In 1982, the minister began leading prayer meetings at St. Nicholas Church in Leipzig on Mondays. The exclusive purpose of the Monday night prayer meetings was to pray for peace. Having grown up in Leipzig during a time when the city was under Communist rule, the pastor knew about the tension among the people and the East German government. Leipzig happened to be his hometown. He studied theology at Karl Marx University. Before the iron curtain fell, it was called the University of Leipzig, a fine school with a long and rich history. He also learned Greek and Latin there. At the same time, he worked summers in a car factory and rode his motorcycle around the city delivering telegrams. He also worked as a train waiter. Through these jobs and his university experience, he could hear what the people were actually saying about the oppression imposed by the Communist government that ruled with an iron hand at that time.

The pastor's name served as a self-fulfilling prophecy. Christian Fuhrer came to be a fitting name for the pastor. Of course, he was a Christian. And in the German language, the term *Fuhrer* means *leader*. The term had been tarnished by the abuse associated with Hitler. Pastor Fuhrer redeemed the term by leading the people to embrace freedom instead of totalitarianism.

Pastor Fuhrer had been influenced as a child by the example set by Jesus. He noticed that Jesus cared for the powerless, the outsiders, and the neglected. As a pastor, he started the prayer meetings with the hope that his church would reflect the care of Christ for the disenfranchised. He dreamed that it could be a place in which the people in Leipzig could talk about and pray for peace. Little did he know when he started the prayer meetings that they would be associated in due time with the collapse of the Berlin Wall.

Starting in 1982, the prayer group met every Monday at his church. The historic Protestant church in the middle of the city became a focal point as the prayer meeting group grew over time. And for Pastor Fuhrer, the prayer meetings helped him to engage his congregants in something that would address the struggles they faced under Communist rule.

In February 1988, the pastor invited fifty people who advocated the right to leave East Germany to join his Monday night prayer groups so they could talk about the issue. About 600 people showed up, including the participants in his prayer group. In May of that year, the police blocked traffic to the church in fear that the crowd had grown too large. When they blocked the traffic, they thought they had put an end to what they feared would be an insurrection.

The barricade didn't stop the people from coming to the church. It had quite the opposite effect. The crowd grew as people attended regularly each Monday night with lighted candles in hand. Pastor Fuhrer encouraged them to carry candles because it would require both hands. With both hands occupied to keep the candles lit while walking, the temptation to pick up a stone and throw it at the police would be diminished.

The Monday night prayer group of a few people grew. One night a crowd of 70,000 people gathered and engaged in a non-violent demonstration. It came to be called the Monday Demonstration on October 9. Pastor Fuhrer urged the people to refrain from violence at the demonstration. Prior to that night, the police had brutalized and threatened the participants who attended the prayer meeting. However, by that time of the October 9 meeting, the police didn't stop it, probably because they couldn't or perhaps they favored the stand the people were taking — a stand regarding the need to be free from Communist rule.

The next Monday night, 120,000 people showed up for the demonstration, candles in hand. Things happened quickly after that night. On November 9, 1989, the Berlin Wall fell.

According to an article in *Ecumenical News International* dated April 30, 2009, the Communist party leader Horst Sindermann lamented the collapse of his government in the wake of the Monday demonstrations. In his lamentation, he confessed, "We were prepared for everything, but not candles and prayers."

Pastor Fuhrer led the people to carry candles and to pray for peace. With the candles in hand, they couldn't give in to the temptation to be violent. With prayers in their hearts, they overcame the fear for their lives. In prayer, they availed themselves to God who would do something new in their hearts.

Some political scholars say what happened wasn't a spiritual renewal. Rather, it was only a political demonstration. When you think about people walking into the face of their fear every Monday night, you have to conclude that their hearts had been stirred, but not by political speeches. Their hearts had been stirred by the Lord who is always eager to do something new among his people if we allow him to do it.

Jeremiah's prophecy promises us that God's in the business of doing something new in the hearts of his people.

It also promises that God's ready to help people have a change of heart, the kind of change that can last into eternity. He is willing to do something about the sin in our hearts.

Through Jeremiah's prophecy, God told the people of Israel that he would forgive their sin and blot out any memory of their sin (v. 34). He made this promise to them in keeping with his pledge to do something new in their hearts. By connecting the removal of sin with the renewal of their hearts, God demonstrated that he considered sin to be a serious problem. Also, he validated his desire to do something about it.

One of the primary leaders of the Protestant Reformation had his struggle with sin to thank for the way God changed his heart. Of course, we are talking about Martin Luther. The awareness of his sin troubled him throughout his young life, and his dread fear of God drove him to find a way to deal with his sin.

On July 2, 1507, for example, he encountered a terrible storm that frightened him into becoming a monk. He devoted himself to being an obedient monk and did everything he could to please God. But all the while, he grieved over his sin. He couldn't find any way out of his sin condition. The law of God convicted him, the wrath of God frightened him, and the righteousness of God angered him. Frustrated, he could hardly endure his awful situation.

Then God in his great mercy pointed Luther to Romans 1:17. There he saw that a righteous person lives by faith. He understood that he couldn't get rid of his sin himself and that Christ has already paid the price for his sin. He grasped that his only response to Christ's gift of salvation was to receive it by faith. That's when he was born again, born from above. His heart was transformed by God's grace in Christ and his response of faith. He lived out Paul's statement that we are saved by grace through faith (Ephesians 2:8).

From that moment, Luther's work took on new meaning. For the next 25 years or so, he devoted himself to proclaiming what it meant to live by faith. His passion for his work got him into more than a little trouble, but he didn't back down or recant. His devotion to God's word prompted him to translate the entire Bible into the German language. Although he spent his life in the little town of Wittenberg, his influence was felt all over Europe. In time other reformers would join him in his work.

What prompted him to make such a monumental impact on his world? Was it a desire to leave a legacy? Was it selfish ambition? Was it awareness that he had a unique message that people wanted to hear? No! He was moved by the Christ who had forgiven his sins and had transformed his heart in the process.

In fact, history shows that many reformers didn't set out to make names for themselves. Like Luther, they simply wanted to share God's gracious message of salvation by faith in Christ. Their Christ-centered message sparked a firestorm time and again in the hearts of people who listened to them. By pointing sinners to Jesus as the only way of salvation, they kindled a spiritual fire that swept their land.

Again, why did they share such a flammable message? Only one reason makes sense. They had experienced the radical change of heart associated with God's grace and mercy in forgiving them of their sins, blotting them from his memory forever. They were compelled to pass the gospel of Christ along to others who ached over their sin as well.

The reformation that gave Martin Luther a place in history books wasn't confined to his native land. It spread beyond the borders of Germany to other parts of Europe. Soon evidences of it showed up in Great Britain. Preachers in that country began to proclaim salvation by grace through faith, and the result was a spiritual awakening that shook that part of the world. In due time, the message of spiritual transformation made its way to the new land of America, and with it came revival. From one coast to the next, the grace of God shown in Jesus Christ has set people free from their sins.

Spiritual transformation isn't only something we talk about in past tense. It's a present reality in many parts of the world today. News from Central and South America, for example, gives us encouragement that the good news of Christ has invaded nations that have been closed by political decree. In Asia and Africa, growing numbers of people are experiencing spiritual transformation as the gospel of Christ is being presented. Other places around the world report the same good news.

Here in the United States, reports of spiritual awakening in some of our cities have been circulating for a while now. God has been changing hearts and transforming lives in places in which we thought he would have given up long ago.

Now to the questions before us. On this Reformation Sunday, what can we say about what God is doing among us? Is God showing that he's doing something among us that's making an eternal difference to anyone?

God's always in the business of doing something new among his people. And we are his people through Jesus Christ. Amen.

The Lamb

Have you ever heard of a man named Polycarp? Don't feel badly if you haven't. Polycarp's not exactly a household name, at least in most houses.

Yes, it's an odd name, to our ears anyway. The name conjures up for most people today a product that's manufactured from something made of plastic that tastes like freshwater fish. In the history of the church, the name lived through one century after another, and the person who bore it gave good reason for people to keep on mentioning the name.

Because of the story behind the name, Polycarp has significance for us as we worship. It's a name rich in meaning when we think about the Christians who died as martyrs. They died because they devoted themselves exclusively to Jesus Christ. John had them in mind when he wrote about the Lamb. He wrote about people in white robes gathering around Jesus Christ, the Lamb of God, and worshiping him.

For that reason, the name Polycarp signifies the value of All Saint's Day. It's the name of a martyr who died for his faith a long time ago. Polycarp happened to be a remarkable man who laid down his life as a testimony of his devotion to Christ. Hopefully the name will live a little longer in our memories because we spent some time retelling Polycarp's story. We hope that retelling his story will give us fresh inspiration to worship the Lord whose love for us compelled many believers down through the centuries to face death because of their love for him.

Polycarp died in about AD 150 in the city of Smyrna. Yes, that's a long, long time ago in a land far, far away. But the significance of that time and place lies in the obvious fact that he died just a little over a century or so after Christianity got off to a good start, thanks to Pentecost.

Church historians say that Polycarp was probably one of John's disciples. You may recall that John had a brother named James, and they were sons of Zebedee. Jesus called them sons of thunder, probably because they were boisterous men who acted like bulls in a china shop when they got out of control, which may have been quite often. Not long after Pentecost, James was murdered. Until his murder, he served as the leader of the church in Jerusalem. But then Herod had him killed (Acts 12:2).

James didn't live very long after the birth of the church, but his brother, John, lived much longer. Some scholars speculate that he may have been around ninety years old or so when he died. He had a long life all right, but no one would say that he had an easy life. Quite the contrary, he had a tough life. He had the privilege of spending many of his years doing hard labor on the island of Patmos, apparently because he worshiped Jesus Christ instead of Caesar. Fortunately for us, that's when the Lord showed him what the future would hold for Christians, and he wrote it down for us in the book of Revelation. The story in that grand Bible centers on the Lamb. The story of the Lamb intersects the story of Polycarp. And their stories intersect our stories as we worship the Lamb ourselves.

Most scholars say that John was the last of the twelve original apostles to die. His life came to an end at about the same time that the first century AD came to a close. Somewhere along the way, perhaps in his last years, he met Polycarp and discipled him in the Christian faith. Apparently he mentored Polycarp well. Many years later his disciple would stand strong in the face of persecution that threatened the lives of Christians everywhere at that time. John had taught his disciple well how to be courageous in the face of death because of his faith in Christ.

As Roman persecution of Christians became more intense in the world in which Polycarp lived, he had an impression that he would face it one day. He even told a friend about having a strange dream about it. In the dream, he saw himself being burned alive for his faith in Christ.

Before long, his dream came true. In due time, the opponents of his faith came for him because he held firm to his conviction that Christians worship Jesus, God's Son, and not Caesar. They intended to bring him and his testimony of Jesus to an end.

When Polycarp heard that his oppressors had come in search of him, he responded simply by praying for God's will to be done. His prayer served as a striking prelude to the memorable testimony he bore as he faced his death unafraid and with complete confidence in Christ.

When they captured him, they never expected to see such an old man. He was quite elderly in their eyes. Perhaps he reminded some of them of their own fathers or grandfathers. Perhaps the notion of executing such an old man made some of them begin to reconsider what they were about to do to him.

They never expected the treatment they received from him once they captured him. They probably didn't know what to do when he made arrangements for them to be given something to eat and drink while he spent some time in prayer. For two hours his executioners sat at his table and ate his food and listened as he talked with God. What they heard in his conversation with the Lord moved them deeply.

According to the record of the event, some of them gave up on persecuting believers and became Christians themselves.

Polycarp's act of kindness turned out to be as extreme as his age. What do you think he must have said in his prayer to render that kind of response from his captors? And think about the confidence and compassion that blended together in his prayer and provision for them. No wonder that some of his captors couldn't go through with his execution.

The time came for him to be taken to the stadium. By the time they arrived with him, the stadium was filled with people who came to watch him die. As his captors led him into the stadium, all of them heard someone say, "Be strong, Polycarp. Be a man!" Although they all heard a voice, they never saw the person who spoke. For that reason, many Christians believed that an angel had appeared to encourage Polycarp as he faced his death.

As he stood before the judge appointed to sentence him to death, Polycarp refused to recant his faith in Christ. The judge tried to frighten him with threats of a cruel death if he chose to hold on to his commitment to Jesus, but he couldn't strike fear in Polycarp. Then he tried to cajole the old, faithful servant of Christ by promising to release him if he would disown Jesus. Polycarp replied by saying that for 86 years Jesus had been faithful to him. In turn, he would remain faithful to the Lord who had saved him.

With that testimony, Polycarp sealed his fate. The judge sentenced him to death, and his executioners decided to burn him alive. They piled up the wood for the fire and tied him to a stake in the middle of the woodpile. As he prepared to die, he prayed. He thanked God for the privilege of dying for him and for the honor of joining other martyrs who had laid down their lives for him as well. He went on to ask for God to be glorified in the person of his Son, Jesus Christ.

When he finished his prayer, his executioners set the wood on fire. According to the account of the story recorded in *The Apostolic Fathers*, the blazing furnace couldn't consume his body. Instead of the nauseating odor of burning flesh, the air was filled with the scent of precious perfume that permeated the stadium. Eventually life left him when a baffled and angry executioner stabbed him with a knife.[1]

Everything Polycarp had said about following Jesus throughout his life had been demonstrated in the way that he faced his death. All of the people he taught as bishop of Smyrna would have the lessons he passed along to them reinforced with the image of him praying for the people who would execute him. They would never forget the way he ended his long life as a loyal, faithful follower of his precious Lord.

Now you know why Polycarp deserves our attention today. His story reminds us of others who laid down their lives for Christ across the centuries. Even today, stories leak out of closed countries about Christians who suffer and die because they won't recant their allegiance to Jesus. Like Polycarp, they lay down their lives willingly like lambs to be slaughtered.

According to the image that John has given us in Revelation 7, such remarkable people will gather in heaven to worship the Lamb, Jesus Christ, God's precious Son, our Savior and Lord. Imagine the scene: lambs slaughtered worshiping the Lamb slain for them. Words cannot express the mood, the character, and the quality of that worship experience.

Throughout the Bible, the gentle lamb has been used to describe some of the most moving features of our relationship with God. Starting with the first Passover meal, the lamb has been associated with sacrifice. In Exodus 12, the gripping account of God's people getting ready to step toward the promised land and their freedom from slavery included a lamb. The lamb's blood sprinkled over the door post of a home spared God's people from the horrible fate that awaited the Egyptian families that night. From that night on, the lamb symbolized God's hand on his people to protect them.

When the Lord met His people on Mount Sinai not long after he liberated them, he made a covenant with them. He instructed them regarding some fairly specific acts of worship. Engaging in the acts of worship that God mandated helped them as they grew in their walk with him. One particularly important act of worship involved sacrificing a lamb. Once each year, on the Day of Atonement, the priest offered a lamb on the altar to express the desire of God's people to be forgiven of their sins. The lamb came to symbolize the sacrifice necessary for God's people to be forgiven and the grace and mercy God showed them by forgiving them.

Little wonder, therefore, that the Old Testament prophets used the image of the lamb when they talked about God's Anointed One who would come and bring deliverance with him. For Israel, therefore, the lamb came to embody what they looked for in God's Messiah. In their portrayals, the prophets pointed out that the Messiah would be treated like a lamb led to the slaughter for us all (Isaiah 53:7).

Centuries later, John the Baptist came along preaching that the Messiah would be coming soon. He warned people to prepare for the arrival of God's Anointed One by repenting of their sins. One day, while he was talking with some of his disciples, he saw Jesus approaching him. Drawing the attention of his disciples to Jesus, John declared him to be the Lamb of God who would take away the sins of the world (John 1:29). Of course, the imagery expressed in the title John conferred on Jesus gave a striking prelude to his life, death, and resurrection.

Just as John said, Jesus was the Lamb of God, and he demonstrated it by the way he lived, died, and rose from the grave. After God's ascension, his disciples proclaimed the good news about his sacrifice for sins. They also began to portray God as a victorious ruler who would come for his people, gathering them from the four corners of the earth to join him in heaven. There God will be the eternal centerpiece of worship. The picture painted with John's words gives us a glimpse into the scene involving the Lamb being worshiped by gentle lambs like Polycarp.

In his Revelation portrayal, John leaves us with another compelling image of Jesus. Not only is he the Lamb to be worshiped, but he is also the Shepherd to be followed. Until the day comes for us to join Polycarp and others who have given themselves to Christ, we can count on Jesus to be our Good Shepherd. According to John 10:11, that's the way Jesus described himself in his relationship with us. That's the way we can think about him until he comes for us.

As our Shepherd, Jesus walks with us while we face our own trials and tribulations because of him. Our distinctive walk with God sets us apart from people around us. Our values don't always allow us to blend in with the crowd, and we have to face the trouble that comes from being different. But Jesus, our Shepherd, walks with us along the way. We are not alone.

When Polycarp walked toward his martyrdom, a voice called out to him to be courageous, but no one could identify the voice. Let's suppose that it was the voice of Jesus, the Good Shepherd, encouraging one of his choice servants not to be afraid. That notion would make sense, given the fact that a shepherd never leaves his sheep. When one of his lambs gets into trouble, the shepherd's never far away. He comes to the rescue. For Polycarp, he came to the rescue, giving his servant what he couldn't give himself in his time of tremendous need.

Many other Christians have heard the voice of the Good Shepherd. No, they didn't stand before tribunals or courageously stake their claim in Christ and die because of their unwillingness to disown him. But they have stood in the face of great pain just the same. They have endured the torture of suffering associated with their bodies wasting away because of terminal diseases. They have agonized over the fate of the people they love at the hands of others who treated them with injustice. They have grieved their losses and for a long time heard nothing but silence when they asked God why they had to lose so much.

None of these people, sweet saints of God, ever gave any impression that they stopped trusting him. Instead, they kept on whispering the verses they memorized as children, kept on humming the tunes of the hymns that sustained them, and kept on believing that although they may be like lambs to the slaughter, they looked forward to beholding the Lamb of God, Jesus Christ, their Messiah. Somehow, they believed that he would come to their rescue.

How can they be so resilient in the face of such torment? Jesus, the Good Shepherd, walks with them. And he walks with us. Either he takes our pain away, or he takes us away from our pain. After all, he knows what it's like to be a lamb. Amen.

---

1. J.B. Lightfoot, *The Apostolic Father* (Grand Rapids, Michigan: Baker Book House, 1983), pp. 109-117.

Proper 27
Pentecost 25
Ordinary Time 32
Joshua 24:1-3a, 14-25

Choosing

Do you remember the generation gap that existed between you and your parents when you were a teenager? Do you sense the same kind of gap widening between you and your children?

When we consider the story of Joshua in his old age calling on Israel to serve the Lord, we have to factor in the reality of a generation gap. It presents a challenge for people of different generations when they try to communicate with each other. Parents who grew up in the seventies and eighties regularly have difficulty talking with their children who are growing up at the beginning of the twenty-first century. Grandparents who grew up in the fifties and sixties have an even tougher time communicating with them.

A generation gap existed between Joshua and the people when he called them to Shechem for a meeting. God had used Joshua to lead the people to take the land God promised them. Now that they had settled in to the land, they had to take responsibility for the lives they would establish there. Joshua had lived with the generation of God's people before them. He was very young when they walked into the desert and crossed the Red Sea on the way to freedom. He remembered well the events that led to God ordering them to wander in it for the rest of their days. He could never forget that they meandered through the desert for their lifetime because they didn't trust God enough to obey him when they had the opportunity.

Standing before the next generation of God's people at Shechem, Joshua could see what kind of people they had become, spiritually speaking, and he wanted to drive home an important point in their minds and hearts. He wanted them to understand clearly that they needed to devote themselves exclusively to God.

However, the generation of God's people who joined him at Shechem didn't have all of Joshua's life experiences to help them. Although they knew the story of the desert, they owned for themselves the dream of taking the land God promised their forefathers, and the hard work associated with making the dream come true. For many of them, what happened in the desert decades earlier came to them as distant, secondhand information. The lack of firsthand experience with God in the desert concerned Joshua. He could see what they lacked in their walk with God would have a negative influence on the choices they would make in the future.

Another issue just as important as the generation gap has to be brought up before we dive into the story told in Joshua 24. The issue in mind has to do with the relationships we nurture across the years. Some people say that all of us give attention to at least four basic relationships throughout our lives: our relationship with God, our relationship with ourselves, our relationship with others, and our relationship with what's around us, or in other words, our relationship with things. Each of these relationships takes some of our time and demands a certain portion of our energies. Figuring out which relationship matters most can be tricky.

Nurturing the relationships that matter most requires us to make tough choices. People who grow up spiritually learn how to make wise choices in these relationships. Unfortunately, some people don't invest the time necessary to make the best choice. In fact, some people can't bring themselves to make a choice at all. For that reason, they appear to be aimless and restless, and they can't seem to find the right path. For them, the toughest part of living has to do with making choices in their relationships.

When Joshua called God's people to meet him at Shechem, he intended for them to make a choice that pertained to the most important relationship of all — a relationship with God. If they made a wise choice in that basic relationship, they would do well. But if they made a poor choice, all of the other relationships in their lives would be affected.

Today we still have been challenged to make a wise choice when it comes to our most critical relationship. Thankfully, we have been given in the New Testament the rest of the story about God's ways with us to help with that critical decision. The New Testament tells the story of God's Son, Jesus Christ, who invites us to choose him. He made choosing him appealing because on the cross he heralded the truth that he chose us. In other words, he invites us to choose him because he chose us first. Before creation was on God's mind, we were on his mind. He loved us since before we knew his name, and he compels us to love him, and he even shows us how to express our love for him by loving others. Choosing to devote ourselves to God opens the door for nurturing healthy relationships with ourselves, other people, and the things he has given us in the world.

Standing there long ago with the people of Israel at Shechem, Joshua helps us today to make a wise choice about nurturing a relationship with God. Notice in particular how he encourages us to study the options and to allow the facts to guide us to make the right choice.

Immediately after he called the people of Israel to the meeting, he reviewed for them the actions God had taken on behalf of their forefathers in fulfillment of his promise to his people (Joshua 24:3-13). He started by reminding them of what God had done in the lives of Abraham, Isaac, and Jacob. Then he went on to remind everyone that God had sent Moses and Aaron to deliver his people from Egyptian bondage. From there, he recalled the events associated with the children of Israel arriving in the promised land and enabling them to occupy the territory so they could live there.

What if they compared what the living God had done for them with the benefits they had received from the lifeless idols to which they had been introduced by their parents? Throughout their lives, they had encountered a number of deities whose names and reputations they knew well. Back in Egypt, their parents had warmed up to a few idols for themselves, and they had brought them along with them. They kept them nearby in their travels in the desert. Now their children possessed them.

With his declaration about what God had done for his people, Joshua challenged everyone at Shechem to scrutinize the idols they kept as heirlooms. What had they enabled the people of Israel to accomplish? Had they been kind and generous to the people in their travels? Had they provided anything for them at all? Had they delivered on their promise to provide the people with a land to call their own? Could God's people testify that they had been sincere and truthful to them?

What the children of Israel knew well, we know even better because of Jesus Christ. Our Savior has shows his unconditional love for us by coming to us, dying for us, rising from the grave for us, and ascending into heaven to prepare a place for us. Right now he abides in us as we abide in him as his friends. Because of God's presence in our lives, we can face whatever life throws at us. For us, he alone deserves all of the honor and glory and dominion now and forever. Indeed, there is no other name greater than the name of Jesus.

It's almost like Joshua was saying to the people, "Look around. Name another object of our worship that will measure up to God in your lives. Find another source of contentment like God. You'll see that you can't. The facts won't allow us to come and see it any other way. God alone has been the source of your victory, and he alone needs to be the object of your devotion."

Having weighed the option, Joshua shows us next how to register our choice. With his classic statement, "Choose you this day," he suggests the value of making our choice and registering it in the presence of others. With his declaration, "As for me and my house, we will serve the Lord," he gives us an example to follow when we think about how to register our choice to give ourselves to Jesus.

Therein lies the problem many of us face with choices in general. We have a tough time making them. With options before us and the best choice right in front of us, we hesitate to choose. We can't settle into a decision. Our indecision becomes our decision, and the choice we make not to decide leaves us aimless and restless, constantly wavering between the options but never being able to nail down our choice.

In worship we have an opportunity to make our choice and nail it down in our hearts. As we sit in our pews in worship services, we can breathe a prayer of commitment to the Lord, saying after his people whom Joshua challenged to make up their minds, "We will serve the Lord!" In our times of private worship we can register our willingness to let the Lord have our lives. In our Bibles we can jot down the date and the time when we registered our choice.

Perhaps you have already made your choice, and you smile quietly as you reflect on the value of registering it in worship. Maybe you've set your heart on the Lord in a quiet place at a time that will always remain one of the critical turning points of your life. However, you could still be wavering in the sea of indecision, tossed back and forth. The time has come for you to say, "I will serve the Lord."

Lauren made her choice not long ago, and she made it known to her family at dinner one night. For a long time, she had struggled with the place the Lord had in her life. As a sixteen-year-old girl, her relationships with others mattered more to her than her relationship with God. When she got closer to seventeen, for some reason her attention began to shift to her relationship with Jesus Christ.

One of Lauren's closest friends at school lived in a way that showed that a relationship with Jesus can be rewarding, fulfilling, and promising. Her friend had erased all of the stereotypes about Christians that she had created in her mind.

One day after school, she asked her friend about how to know Jesus personally. Her friend showed her the way to a personal walk with God, and Lauren took it from there. She prayed by her bedside that night, giving her life to Christ.

The next evening at dinner, Lauren told her family about her decision. Because they made their decision to follow the Lord years earlier, her parents were pleased. Lauren never forgot that night when she registered her commitment to follow Christ.

The story about Joshua gathering the people of Israel at Shechem shows us something else about choices. He demonstrates for us the value of investing in our choice to follow Christ. Registering our choice confirms our decision to give our lives to the Lord, but investing in our choice helps us to live out the choice we have made.

That's probably why Joshua said he didn't think that God's people would live out the decision they had registered in his presence. He remembered a time a generation ago when God's people made a similar decision.

After the Lord had shown the people his power by delivering them from Egypt and enabling them to walk on dry land to the freedom side of the Red Sea, he called them to join him at Mount Sinai. There they heard from Moses the good news about the covenant that God wanted to affirm with them. Immediately they signed on for themselves, and they rejoiced over their choice and the fact that God had given them the opportunity to make it.

When God called Moses to the mountain, however, things changed radically. His people who said they would devote themselves exclusively to him just a few weeks earlier changed their minds in a flash. In keeping with their decision, they tasked Aaron with the chore of creating another deity for them. Once he fashioned a god favorable to them, they ditched the living God altogether.

Why did they regress to idol worship? Why didn't they live out their decision to worship and serve the Lord God alone? The answer lies in part in the fact that they hadn't made an investment in their decision. They made their choice, but they hadn't made it a part of their lives.

Joshua saw what happened when Moses finally came down from the mountain. The scene left him with the distinct conviction that when people make their decision to follow the Lord, they need to take their commitment seriously.

How do we reflect the reality that we take our walk with God seriously? We invest in our decision, and we do it in way that's simple to understand but sometimes difficult to put into practice. We embrace God's ways and determine that we will live according to them. We take his word seriously, for in the scriptures we learn about his ways with us. We take prayer seriously too, but in conversation with God we gain what we need in order to live out our commitment to him. Furthermore, we take each other as siblings in Christ seriously. We regard each other as fellow strugglers who walk together with Christ to take on kingdom tasks in our community, around the world, and everywhere in the middle.

Perhaps Joshua could see the potential for disaster in the faces of the people he addressed that important day at Shechem. They responded too flippantly, without any regard for how they intended to make consistent investments in the decision they had just registered. For that reason, he guided them to make their first investment in their decision. He wrote in a book the commitment they had made, and he placed a rock under a tree to remind them of their pledge. Every time they passed that way, they would remember what they said. The rock would hold them accountable for their choice.

The sad truth is that God's people turned out to do exactly as Joshua predicted. According to Judges 2:11, the people broke their promise to God not long after Joshua died. And they had to live with the choice they made.

The story presents us with the challenge to grow in our relationship with God by studying the options, registering our choice, and investing in the decision we have made. When we do, we can count on God to give what we need in order for us to live according to his ways. Amen.

Powerless People

Some time ago, someone in Fred's congregation asked him to read a book by a fellow named Tex Sample. As pastor of the church, Fred always appreciated the opportunity to read books recommended by his congregants. His long years of ministry had taught him that in almost every book he could find at least one good idea. Sometimes the idea would find its way into one of his sermons. At other times, the idea would be tucked away for further examination, or it would be presented over coffee to engage the people gathered around the table in a hearty conversation or debate.

He thanked the parishioner for sharing about the book to him, and he agreed to read the book at his first opportunity. He took the book to his study and placed it on his desk. A couple of weeks later he picked it up and started to read it. The subtitle captured his attention immediately.[1] He wondered what a book about Will Rogers, Uncle Remus, and Minnie Pearl would be about, and he pondered for a moment the meaning of oral culture.

Not too many pages into the book, however, he began to see what oral culture meant, and he could begin to understand how the people identified in the subtitle fit into what Sample was trying to say.

The more pages Fred turned, the more he could see himself in the book. He had been brought up in a family composed of people who had earned their living by hard work. Later on, he would discover that Sample had a name for such folks. Sample referred to them as hard-living people.[2] Blue-collar

63

folks, they had never really been given a chance to rise above their hard-living ways.

Fred always considered himself to be one of the most fortunate people in the world. Brought up in near-poverty, he never dreamed as a young boy that he would get a college education, much less a seminary degree that would enable him to post "Dr." in front of his name.

Of course, he had a number of people to thank for his educational achievement. His mother encouraged him, even though she didn't have any money to give toward Fred's education. With four brothers and two sisters, Fred never intended his parents to pay for his college education anyway. In his last year in high school, he had learned about student grants, and he was able to take advantage of them and the student loans that were made available to him.

And he knew how to work. His dad had taught him that hard work gave a man respectability. Fred found out soon enough that it would also give a university student an income. He worked at night and went to class during the day. Somewhere in between he studied for tests and wrote papers required by his professors and found time to rest.

At seminary he really flourished. His professors taught him how to think and write theologically, and they instilled in him a love for books and articles that stretched him academically. He always looked on his days at seminary with fondness and gratitude.

The day he defended his dissertation was a crowning moment in his academic life, but it proved to be a painful experience too. After he defended his dissertation for a couple of hours before a panel of professors, they invited him to step into the hallway so they could deliberate and come to a decision about what he had written. A short time later, one of his professors escorted him back into the room. There he saw the professors standing, a signal at his seminary that his dissertation had passed. Later that day, he called his dad to tell him the good news. His heart broke when his dad replied to his announcement with one curt question, "So, when are you going to get a job?" His dad's reply made the day bittersweet. He knew in his mind that his dad didn't have any use for education, but in his heart Fred hoped that he would transcend his mistrust of degrees and affirm his son's work. But he didn't.

That day hadn't faded from his memory when he sat in his study and read Sample's book. But reading the book helped him to gain a helpful perspective on his dad, his own background, his family, his ministry, and his congregation.

With his eyes opened to the cultural phenomenon that Sample called orality, Fred went on to read about people who prefer to relate to their world using what they see, hear, and say instead of what they read and write. Their preference for oral communication affects how they relate to other people. As Fred read on, he identified with the description of oral people rendered in the pages of the book. Moreover, he could understand why they behaved that way.

He knew from experience that they usually have little or no power in society. Because of their powerlessness and the mistreatment they receive at the hands of powerful people, they grow suspicious of anything that resembles power over them. An education is something that most of them don't have, and they don't really trust a person who's earned degrees or who talks using words they don't normally use in their own discourse. Fred's father's question made sense to him when he thought about it in light of what he had read.

His mind had been trained well at seminary. Having grasped the reality that people all over the world favor power and long to be powerful themselves, the whole notion of powerless people had the ring of truth for him. He asked himself about how many of the people in his church would consider themselves powerless.

Then he began to reflect on Jesus' popularity with the people, and the idea struck him that they crowded to hear Jesus because they found in him something that enabled them to transcend their powerless existence. Most of them probably couldn't read or write, and they likely had little chance to rise above their poverty-stricken circumstances. In the presence of Jesus, however, the political leaders and the religious leaders of the day didn't seem to be so threatening to them. They felt as if people with power wouldn't hurt them as long as they were near him.

Like Fred came to realize for himself, powerless people live all around us, and hopefully they go to church with us. In the fellowship of other believers, they shouldn't have to be afraid of someone hurting them. At church they should feel safe.

Who would be on your list of powerless people today? Like Sample indicated in his book, people who are illiterate or functionally illiterate make their way to the list. Some of them can't read and write at all. Others can read and write enough to fill out applications, but that's about all. According to a recent census, people who are either illiterate or functionally illiterate compose about 50% of the population of the United States.[3] Odds are that they live in our community, and hopefully they attend our church. Powerless or nearly powerless in a culture empowered by what's printed on paper, they should find a place in church in which they can have an encounter with God even though they can't read the Bible very well.

Let's compare what Fred learned with the story in Judges 4. In the story, we meet Deborah and Barak. Both of them would likely be on the list of powerless people but not necessarily because they couldn't read or write very well. They were powerless just the same, and they lived in a world in which they had to deal with powerful oppressors.

Deborah lived in a land and at a time when she had no power whatsoever. For one thing, she happened to be a woman. In those days, being a woman gave her only a slight advantage over being a cow or a donkey. In fact, cows and donkeys may have mattered more than women in some of the homes back then.

Her powerlessness also resulted from the fact that she considered herself a citizen of the nation of Israel. According to the book of Judges, being an Israelite didn't mean much in terms of power at that time and in that land. The nation of Israel seemed to be easily kicked around by oppressive enemies.

Like the story in Judges 4 indicated, the leaders of Israel deserved to be kicked around a little. They had a bad habit of getting themselves into trouble because of bad judgment in their relationship with God. Their trouble always stemmed from the same horrible mistake. They repeatedly made the awful mistake of forgetting about the living God who had guided them to the land in which they had settled. That's when they would be vulnerable to the enemy tribes living around them that wanted to do them in at one time or the other.

When the oppression from their enemies made them buckle, the people of Israel would always cry out to the Lord and beg him to help them. Of course, he would come to the rescue by sending a judge, which was really more like a military leader, to deliver them from their oppressors. For a little while after their liberation, they would walk with the Lord. Eventually, however, they would repeat the same mistake again and again and again.

Deborah, an Israelite woman, represents powerless people who live and work in our community. Remember that powerless people know they may never get out of the rut that hard living and injustice has placed them. Their circumstances make for an oppressive environment in which

67

to live. They have few or no choices, and they live at the mercy of powerful people more than they would like to admit, but they can't find a way to get a better choice for themselves.

You may consider yourself a powerless person like Deborah, but again, not because you can't read very well or because of some other reason. You may feel that you've got few choices in life. Or you may feel that you have to contend with oppressive people or entities that have the power to force you to do things against your will. If that's the case, you can identify with Deborah.

Barak's not much better off than Deborah. Granted, he's a man, but that's about all we can say about his power over Deborah in that day. Interestingly enough, the writer of Hebrews mentioned him as an example of faith (Hebrews 11:32). When we read the whole story of Deborah and Barak, we would agree that he deserved to be on that elite list. When we read the song that he and Deborah sang about the Lord's deliverance, we would agree with one obvious observation (Judges 5). Both of these powerless people tapped into a source of power that can inspire us if we tap into it as well.

According to the story, Deborah tapped into the rich resource of a personal relationship with God, which empowered her to do something incredible. Apparently, her walk with God rendered credibility for her among her neighbors. They trusted her to give them wise counsel, so apparently they sought her out to help them find their way. In fact, the place where people met her eventually came to bear her name. Deborah's palm tree stood out as the place where people could find her if they wanted to draw from the deep well of her wisdom. Over time, her wisdom produced for her a fair amount of credibility, but her walk with God nurtured courage in her. She was so courageous that she didn't hesitate to consider the reality that God may speak to her.

Don't overlook what's happened in the story. A powerless person has been empowered by a relationship with God. It happened then, and it can happen now. He can make us wise, and he can instill courage within us too.

Also, don't underestimate the enemy in the story. The Canaanite army had been oppressing Israel for twenty years, and the oppression had been brutal. The army had acquired the latest instruments of war: iron chariots. In fact, they owned 900 of them, and they used them in their torment of Israel. As you could imagine, the swords and spears of the men of Israel were no match for the sophisticated, tank-like chariots that proved to be unstoppable. With such advanced instruments for battle and an instinct for uncivilized treatment of weak people and nations, the Canaanites had nothing or no one to stop them in their torment of Israel. Indeed, the Canaanite army was a formidable foe.

Yet, God turned out to be stronger. Through Deborah and Barak, he destroyed the army and liberated his people. Imagine that: the powerless nation of Israel defeated the cold-hearted and powerful Canaanites. How did they do it? God worked through them to give them what they could not give themselves so they could overcome. Of course, they enjoyed the victory over the Canaanites because they obeyed the Lord. They trusted God to be faithful to his people and powerful enough to protect them when they turned to him.

The message in this story has a number of applications for us today. In fact, it can be directed to three groups of people, all of whom may be listening to this sermon.

First, if you have power over people, use it wisely. Imitate God by directing your power to help people under your authority and not to hurt them. If you use it to abuse powerless people, you have to realize that you will be held accountable for your actions. You may think the powerless will have no recourse, but the Lord who loves them won't sit idly by for long. Just ask the Canaanites.

Second, if you have the ability and you want to make a difference in the life of a powerless person, then don't wait around any longer to do something. Get started now. Do something, anything. Yes, help adults who can't read or write to learn those important skills. That's only one example. Do anything else that will empower them to rise above their helplessness. But most of all, give attention to helping them have a personal relationship with God through Jesus Christ. Empowering them involves spiritual as well as occupational and relational issues. Tend to all of them as you empower them.

Third, if you find yourself to be powerless and living at the mercy of others, remember that the Lord gives strength to the weak. Rest assured that no oppressor can stand against him. God will enable you to know his wisdom and to walk in his ways. Accordingly, God will work through and in you in ways that will surprise you. So turn to him. And don't forget the question that the apostle Paul raised in Romans 8:31: If God's for us, who would dare be against us? And don't forget the answer either: nobody. Amen.

---

1. Tex Sample, *Ministry in an Oral Culture: Living with Will Rogers, Uncle Remus, and Minnie Pearl* (Louisville, Kentucky: Westminster/John Knox Press, 1994).
2. Tex Sample, *Hard-Living People and Mainstream Churches* (Nashville, Tennessee: Abingdon, 1993).
3. Sample, *Ministry in an Oral Culture*, 6.

God Cares

Imagine yourself in a remote location, separated from familiar faces and places. The location could be a city teeming with people, but nobody there knows you or cares to know you. Or maybe it's a lonesome wasteland in which you are separated from another human being by scores of miles. The distance — either geographical or relational — creates an unforgiving barrier between you and interaction with others. Not a pretty picture so far. Lonely. Isolated. Separated.

Now imagine that you have been placed in that remote location against your will. You were forced to go to the strange and awful place that feels like a cold, dank prison. Being there reminds you of the warm, inviting home you were forced to leave. Leaving everything that you associate with home, you have been given no other choice but to start over in this strange place. You won't get any help from your new surrounding. Don't count on anyone to check on you from time to time. Forget about being loved and nurtured. Survive if you can. If you can't, then you'll die lonely and alone.

Into this imaginary scene, add one more important detail. You haven't heard from God ever since you arrived. Like every other person who believes in the living God of the Bible, you want to know him better and walk with him more closely. You have read one passage after the next in the Bible, and you have learned about how much God cares and how you can depend on him to intervene in your time of crisis. Yet, in this particular crisis, he hasn't shown up yet, and he hasn't given much of an impression that he actually cares for you. You wonder if what the Bible says about God is actually trustworthy information.

Maybe for you, the awful predicament described so far isn't the product of your imagination at all. It really exists in your world. It's not far-fetched. Rather, it is a fitting description of your situation right now. The ring of truth for you in the description is that God doesn't seem to care about you where you are right now. You feel like you've been deported to a strange land, and God seems to have lost your forwarding address.

If that's the case for you, then you can identify with the Israelites after they were taken into Babylonian exile. The forced march from Jerusalem to Babylon took them farther and farther from their home each day, and it seemed to take them some distance away from the Lord as well. Their last image of Jerusalem included the walls toppled, the temple destroyed, and the city on fire. Gone, everything was gone. And so were they, to a distant land to start over, presumably all by themselves. God went only as far as the county line. From that point on, they would have to go it alone.

The prophecy we read in Ezekiel 34 must have been welcomed by God's people as they languished in their loneliness in the distant land to which they had been led by their captors. The prophecy reassured them that God still cared, and he expressed his concern for them in some redemptive ways.

We would do well to allow this message in Ezekiel to remind us of God's caring ways with us. Although we may feel distant from him, we can rest assured that our feeling isn't based on facts. The facts in this prophecy point to the reality that God is close and that he cares.

God expresses his care by nourishing his people (vv. 11-16). Notice in the text the number of references to feeding sheep. These references point to one of the ways in which God will take care of the people he loves. He nourishes us.

In Ezekiel's prophecy, God compared the people of Israel in Babylonian exile to a flock of sheep that had been scattered in every direction. Vulnerable because they had been separated from each other, some of the sheep had been abused by predators. Others had gotten lost. All of them had suffered from not having been fed. They suffered from malnourishment. Someone had to step in and help them or they would grow weaker. If they didn't fall victim to a predator, they would eventually starve to death.

Using the setting of Ezekiel as the backdrop, comparing weary Christians to hungry sheep is easy. We understand the analogy at first glance. Like scattered sheep, we sometimes find ourselves lost and alone, spiritually and emotionally impoverished, wondering what to do next. For some of us, our spiritual poverty has turned into a serious form of malnourishment. One of the character traits of such a chronic problem is that we don't even know we are hungry anymore. We have grown so accustomed to the gnawing pain in our soul that we don't even sense it. We have gone so long without any spiritual food that we have lost our taste for it.

In the New Testament, Peter talked about the food. He compared Christians to newborn babies who depended on mother's milk exclusively for their nourishment. He went on to say that believers needed to take in pure spiritual milk (1 Peter 2:1). From what source did such spiritual nourishment come? According to Peter, it came from God's word. A steady diet of his word would give believers what they needed so they could grow strong. And being strong would be critical. The struggles they faced would be taxing, to say the least. They needed to be spiritually well-fed.

God knows that we need his word in order for us to be nourished properly. That's why God has given us his word. By referring to God's word, we draw the conclusion correctly that he's talking about the Bible. Taking time to read and meditate on the Bible feeds us spiritually. When we give attention to the scripture, one outcome can be guaranteed. We will be drawn to Jesus Christ, whom John called the word of life (1 John 1:1). Through the written Word, we grow in our relationship with the living word. In that relationship we find the nourishment we need.

What does the provision of God's word say about him? It says that God cares about us enough to feed us. And he nourishes us in the best way possible. He feeds us in a personal relationship with God through Jesus Christ, a relationship described well in his written word. It's a wonderful expression of his care for us.

God also expresses his care by judging his people (vv. 16, 20-22). At first glance, you may wonder how God's judgment could be an expression of his care. We generally tend to think about God's judgment in terms of a foreboding legal action taken against people who have not taken him seriously. For the people being judged, such a perspective is correct. But for the people who have been victimized by the injustices of predators, God's judgment becomes an act of mercy. They see it as a time when injustices cease and predators are held accountable for what they have done to hurt God's people. In that way, judgment shows that God cares.

Ron and Melinda saw judgment in that way when they walked through the ordeal of a trial. Their daughter, Samantha, had been killed by a drunk driver. When they found out that the driver had been driving without a license and that he had been ticketed a number of times for driving drunk, they were enraged. When they saw him try to manipulate the legal system so he would avoid being accountable for Samantha's death, they could hardly contain their fury. As they watched the scene unfold leading up to the trial, they felt that they had been victimized by the slow legal procedure. But they discovered that while it's slow, justice was sure. In due time, the person who took their daughter's life stood before a judge and was pronounced guilty. At that moment, they felt a sense of closure. Justice had been served.

The people of Israel felt helpless as they were herded from their homes to a life of captivity in Babylon. God spoke through the prophet to remind them that he held the leaders of Israel accountable for what had happened to them. The religious leaders had to be held accountable for not leading God's people to nurture a relationship with him. Picking up the comparison between God's people and sheep, the prophet referred to the leaders who misguided Israel as shepherds who didn't care for the flock and who victimized the sheep (vv. 1-10).

In the analogy, the prophet also compared the uncaring leaders to fat sheep (vv. 17-21). Because of their size, they could be spotted easily, especially in a flock of undernourished sheep. Their size reflected the way they had behaved. Like God said, they had pushed the weaker lambs aside in their quest to satisfy their self-indulgence. They got to the food first and didn't care if others were fed. Furthermore, they used their weight to push sheep away from the flock. They goaded the smaller sheep with their horns, eventually driving them from the flock altogether. No wonder so many were famished. No wonder so many had been lost. No wonder the flock had been scattered.

As the Lord promised, judgment day would be coming soon enough. The fat sheep as well as the thin sheep would be judged. That's when the fat sheep would see that their fatness set them apart for slaughter.

In the same way, God's people can count on him to render justice. All people everywhere will be included. No one will be able to escape it. In his justice, people who mistreat his followers will be held accountable. According to Matthew 25, Jesus said that he would return one day and judge the world. He would separate the people who followed him from individuals who had not taken him seriously. His followers would be welcomed in to heaven. The people who rejected God would face the sentence of his punishment. Everyone is included in his judgment, and the issue on which all of us will be judged has been clearly described.

God's justice doesn't always wait that long. He has the final word in people who mistreat others because they follow him, and he will mete out justice to whomever he wishes whenever he wishes. For the judged, it will be awful. For those who have been victimized, it will express the reality that he really cares for the people who have given themselves to him.

God expresses his care in yet another way. He demonstrates it in the way he leads his people (vv. 23-24). He doesn't give up on us, and he provides leadership so we can grow in our relationship with him.

Continuing to use the imagery of sheep to elaborate on God's ways with his people, the prophet proclaimed that they could look forward to the arrival of a new shepherd. Notice the sequence of events heralded by Ezekiel. First, God would nourish his scattered sheep in order to restore them to health. Then God will judge the selfish predators that have mistreated them. Finally, God will raise his shepherd who will guide the sheep.

The prophet provided a captivating description of the shepherd God had in mind. He referred to the shepherd as his servant, David. Later on, he said that David would be a prince among them. Indeed, David was both a shepherd and a prince. His boyhood was spent in the pasture with sheep. As an adult, he wrote about God's goodness by comparing him to a loving and caring shepherd. When God anointed him to succeed Saul as king, he demonstrated a remarkable sense of spiritual maturity. As a prince, so to speak, he lived on the run in the wilderness so he could escape Saul's sword.

In the end, he became a king and served God well. All Israel loved him. Little wonder that the shepherd God had in mind would be a David figure.

From our side of the cross, we affirm that Jesus Christ fit the description of the shepherd God promised his people long ago. Born in Bethlehem from the line of David, Jesus was the fulfillment of the prophecy regarding the Davidic shepherd who would guide God's people. He even referred to himself as the Good Shepherd who would lay down his life for his sheep (John 10:11).

Because of Jesus Christ, another feature of the prophecy was fulfilled. God promised his people through the prophet that he would be their God. In other words, God would take the initiative to restore his relationship with them so they would be able to call on him. God would see to it that they would walk with him and live according to his ways. Jesus made the restoration of that relationship possible. He tore down the wall that our sin built. The wall separated us from God. With the walls tumbling down, an intimate walk with God can begin.

As a result of what Christ has done for us, we have been given the leadership we need for our future. The Lord can be counted on to direct our steps so we will please him with our lives. In pleasing him, we find joy and contentment.

Best of all, the Lord doesn't lead us from a distance. Quite the opposite, God walks with us each step of the way, and he remains intimately involved with us. He challenges us to spend time with him, to listen to him, to trust him, and to obey him. The purpose of these challenges is to help us to follow God faithfully and to grow in him toward spiritual maturity.

Let's return to the beginning. Earlier you were asked to imagine yourself in an isolated place, held there against your will, with no impression that God even cared about you. After working through Ezekiel's prophecy, you can add other important detail to the image created so far. Imagine the Lord observing everything that's going on with you and working in your life to nourish you so you can press on in his name. Imagine God holding accountable the predators in your life who seek to do injustice simply because they are strong and you are weak. Now imagine God leading you out of isolation and toward home where you belong.

Actually, you don't have to imagine it. If you don't already live it, you can by turning to Jesus Christ. He nourishes you, renders justice for you, and leads you. Why? Because God cares for you. Believe it. Act on it. Amen.

Thanksgivings
to Remember

Joan sat on the sofa reflecting on the Thanksgiving Day holiday that she and her children had enjoyed together. Her children and their spouses seemed to enjoy the meal she had prepared, and she couldn't have been happier in the kitchen with them stirring around in the living room and helping out in the kitchen. Most of all, she delighted in having all of her family at home and at her dinner table one more time. Even though her grandchildren seemed to be a little fidgety at times, she was grateful they sat at the table with their parents, and of course, their grandmother.

At Thanksgiving, she missed her husband most. He always looked forward to Thanksgiving, and he planned family things to do all day long so they could make memories. An advocate of crafting memories in the hearts and minds of children that would encourage them when they got older, he took seriously every opportunity to create a memorable moment. What he didn't know was that being with him was memorable enough for Joan and the children. She held back a tear or two as she thought about how he still existed in the memories of the people gathered around the table.

As the day drifted along, Joan noticed something that bothered her as she observed her family. Before the meal, everyone gathered in the living room and drifted to the kitchen to see if they could help with the preparation of the meal. However, if they weren't in the kitchen helping her, they were spending most their time watching a ball game on television, playing computer games, or just talking with each other. After everyone had finished eating, they returned to the same set of activities.

The day before Thanksgiving, she had gone through her normal routine that included reading the morning newspaper while she sipped her morning coffee. An article about Thanksgiving caught her attention. She had read an article like it before. In fact, almost every Thanksgiving edition had a story about how the holiday was born. In the article, she read about a historic presidential decree that called on Americans to set aside a day to offer sincere and humble thanks to God. The detail in the article about thanking God caught Joan's attention. As she reflected on what she had read, she observed her family spending Thanksgiving doing everything but thanking God for his goodness and grace. While they enjoyed what Thanksgiving gave them as a family, they seemed to have forgotten the reason for the holiday.

Moses looked with concern on the people of Israel as they prepared to make their way into the promised land. He knew them well. He had led them for four decades, and he had come to understand how they could rise to the occasion and serve God. He also knew they could shirk their responsibility and forego their relationship with God. As they ventured into the land God would give to them, they needed to be reminded of the conduct God expected of them. In his message in Deuteronomy 8, Moses wanted them to remember how God had blessed them by giving them the land. If they didn't take time to remember and thank God for his blessings, they would forget about what he had done and give themselves the credit for their achievements.

In his message, he followed the simple line of thought. If God's people remembered him, they would bless him and reap the reward that came with expressing their gratitude. However, if they forgot about God, they would suffer the consequences that would always accompany being ungrateful.

Moses' message to God's people then helps us now as we focus our attention on Thanksgiving Day. Like Joan, we may be concerned about our children and grandchildren growing up and forgetting the value of expressing gratitude. We worry about the outcome of an ungrateful family, an ungrateful community, and an ungrateful society. Like Moses, we can see how gratitude can be nurtured and how it can be overlooked.

Like Moses said, gratitude to God can be nurtured by remembering what he has done for us (vv. 7-10). In Moses' day, the people of Israel faced a glorious opportunity as they stood at the border of the land God would give to them. When they made the promised land their home, they would enjoy lots of good benefits. They would have plenty of water in the springs and fountains flowing in the hills and valleys. They would have plenty to eat. Grain fields, fruit orchards, and vegetable gardens would abound. They would discover more than enough copper and iron to be mined. Their discoveries would lead them to lack for nothing. Plenty of benefits indeed! Moses insisted that they should take time to remember that God had given the land to them and blessed him for what he had done.

Likewise, God has been good to us. Our nation continues to be a beacon of liberty to all other nations. Our community faces challenges, but we have also been given a number of blessings. Our church has been the beneficiary of God's blessings as well. While we enjoy the blessings God has given us, we should remember to thank him. It's the least we can do in light of his great blessings to us.

As Moses also pointed out, an ungrateful attitude can be fostered by forgetting what God has done for us (vv. 11-18). Notice that Moses warned God's people that forgetting him would have shameful consequences. If they forgot to take God seriously, then they would be on the path of forgetfulness. In time, they would enjoy the blessings God provided without thinking about him at all. They would grow proud and arrogant by deluding themselves that God had nothing to do with the blessings they enjoyed. They would begin to pat themselves on the back. In so doing, they would forget about God's leadership in their lives, his provision for them, and his attention to them while they traveled in the desert. They would forget that God made it possible for them to enjoy the plentiful bounty that he had set before them. In their arrogance, they would set themselves up for the shame that always comes when we forget God.

How can we grow in gratitude so we won't forget God on Thanksgiving Day? Kim may be able to help us. Her experience provides a way forward for us to enjoy what Thanksgiving is all about for Christians.

The semester had already been long enough for Kim. Being a freshman had been tough for her. Adjusting her study habits, coming to terms with professors who didn't know her name and didn't care to learn it, and getting used to dorm life seemed to pale in comparison to her almost constant bouts with homesickness. At night she would cry herself to sleep, thinking about her bed at home and her parents. She even missed her little brother, who had been nothing but a pest to her as far back as she could remember.

Now nothing sounded as good to her as going home. She could hardly wait for Thanksgiving break so she could return to her home for an entire week. That's why her heart sank to the floor after she found out that a trip home at that time would probably not be possible. Term papers at school and a change in plans at home left her with only one option: to drive up to her uncle's home for Thanksgiving Day. The rest of her time would be spent at school in the library or in front of her computer, and in either case, all by herself.

In her anger over what she considered to be unfair treatment, she emailed her mother about the family's change in plans and what it would mean for her situation at school. Kim blamed her for being insensitive and thoughtless. She went on to remind her mother of the favored treatment her little brother had received all of his life, adding that had he been away at school, such a change in plans wouldn't have been considered at all!

Kim pressed the *send* button and sat there in her dorm room with the late afternoon sun casting a sad glow over her sullen face and showing the streaks the tears made as they made tracks of sadness on her cheeks. She waited for a minute and wondered if she had done the right thing. After all, her mom couldn't do anything about the change of plans. Her husband (and Kim's dad) wanted to visit his dad who had been sick for a long time. In fact, the doctors agreed that the past couple of birthdays had not been good to the old gentleman and that no medicine could be prescribed that would stretch out his days. Kim's dad didn't want to live in regret over not making one more visit, and Kim's mom understood completely. That's why she made arrangements for Kim to spend Thanksgiving with her brother and his wife, an uncle and aunt whom Kim loved dearly.

At the moment Kim didn't think about her dad's need to see his dad. She could only think about her agony over needing to see her folks and the home she missed so much.

Two hours had passed before Kim noticed that her mother had replied. She read, "Sweet Kim, I knew that not being home at Thanksgiving would break your heart. And I understand why you are mad at me. But keep in mind that Thanksgiving is about being grateful for what you have, not angry over what you don't have. Try to understand that your dad needs to say good-bye to his dad. Enjoy being with your uncle. They look forward to seeing you. And remember what Thanksgiving Day is all about!"

Kim went to her uncle's home for Thanksgiving, dutifully but not joyfully. The night before Thanksgiving, he invited Kim to join the family in worship at church. Kim reluctantly agreed, but she didn't anticipate anything good would come from the worship experience.

As she sat in the service, she was pleasantly surprised by what the minister said in his sermon. He read Psalm 107, and he invited the congregation to imagine themselves at a worship service in which people gather from all over the world for the sole purpose of thanking God for his goodness and grace.

At this point, consider yourself invited to join Kim and to participate in that worship service too. Yes, imagine people coming from everywhere to thank God for what he had done in their lives. Imagine the worship leader standing at the platform in the worship service and leading the vast congregation to sing joyful songs of thanksgiving. Then, moving the direction of the service toward testimonies, the worship leader asks, "Who would be willing to express your gratitude to God? If the Lord's been good to you, stand up and say so!"

Picture someone in the congregation standing up and talking about the time he and his friends wandered in the wilderness for a long time. In time, their hunger and thirst got the best of them. And despair overwhelmed them. With nowhere else to go, they cried out to God. He came to their rescue and showed them the way home.

A wilderness doesn't have to be literal in order to be awful. You may remember the agony of wandering in a spiritual desert because you lost your way. Then God showed you the way home when you finally turned to him. You owe God a debt of gratitude because he put you on the right path. How do you show him that you are thankful?

In the imaginary worship service created by Psalm 107, turn your attention to some people who had languished in prison because of their own bad choices. They had defied God, and they paid the price for their disobedience by doing time. The misery of their punishment made them beg God for help.

God could have left us in the spiritual prison we built with our disobedience. He could have forgotten about us when we suffered in our slavery to sin. But he didn't. He set us free by paying the price for our liberty with the life of his Son. How do you express your gratitude to him for the freedom you have in Christ?

Next in the worship service came the testimony of some people who had been healed from serious diseases. They were called on next to testify. They had made some foolish choices that showed a deliberate disregard for God's ways. They suffered for their foolishness by putting them at death's door. That's when they turned to the Lord, and he spared them. He restored them to good health and to a life no longer bent on self-destruction.

You may remember a time when you know that God spared your life. The split second that saved you came from God's hand, and you know it. You have never forgotten how your life has been different because God restored your life to you. What have you done to demonstrate to God how grateful you are to him for giving your life back to you?

As the service continued, picture some seafarers who spoke up next. They had seen God's great power in the middle of a fierce storm at sea. Over and over God lifted their ship up high onto the top of a mountain of water. Then God dropped it deep into the yawning valley between the giant swells. Terrified, they cried out to the Lord. That's when they beheld his great mercy. He calmed the storm and led their ship to a safe harbor.

Storms come in different shapes and sizes. Some of them may be literal, and others may be relational, financial, or medical. All of them share one common feature: They scare us nearly to death. No matter how hard we try, we can't stop them. Helpless, all we can do is cry out to God for help. You probably recall when you begged God for help, and he protected you. He calmed your storm and guided you to safety. How have you shown him your gratitude?

Think about the attention of the congregation turning now to you. It's your turn to stand up and testify about God's grace to you in Christ Jesus. If God has reached into your life and made an eternal difference, then express your gratitude to him. If the Lord has redeemed you, then say so.

As Kim listened, she thought about her own testimony of gratitude, and she thanked God for his goodness to her in ways that she had almost forgotten. She thanked him for the unlikely blessing that came from a botched Thanksgiving holiday plan. Otherwise, she may have forgotten the reason for Thanksgiving Day.

We've listened to Joan's story and to Kim's story. What's your story? Is it a story about remembering and being grateful? Let's hope so. Amen.

www.ingramcontent.com/pod-product-compliance
Lightning Source LLC
Chambersburg PA
CBHW072013060426
42446CB00043B/2366